Love Your Job!

Advance Praise for *Love Your Job!*

"An excellent assortment of insights into the psychological and functional barriers to career self expression . . . and encouraging advice for breaking through them."

> Tom Jackson, author of *Guerilla Tactics in the New Job Market*

"A useful perspective on how to relate to the world of work, rooted equally in research and in common sense."

> Howard Gardner, author of *Frames of Mind: The Theory of Multiple Intelligences*

"*Love Your Job!* offers advice which is both practical and inspirational. It is more than just a supplement to traditional job search guides; it explores (and explodes) the myths, stereotypes, and excuses which keep people from finding jobs they can love . . . This is an excellent resource for laymen and career planning professionals alike."

> Kevin Harrington, Director, Career Planning and Placement Office, Harvard University Graduate School of Education

"Some highly practical solutions to finding, keeping, and loving a job."

> Dr. Albert Ellis, author of *A New Guide to Rational Living*; President, Institute for Rational-Emotive Therapy

"Motivational, inspirational, as good for a person with a job as without one."

> Frank Cullen, President, Keystone Associates

"A practical, uplifting career guide, brimming with sound knowledge and inspiration."

> Christine Melchior, Career Consultant

"The career book for the 90's. Here's the new definition of 'corporate loyalty.' "

> Barry Coughlin, Manager, Educational Services, VMark

"Chock-full of extremely useful tips for job seekers. I recommend Dr. Powers' book to anyone starting out or changing careers."

> Joan M. Stoia, Director, Mather Career Center, University of Massachusetts

"This is no garden-variety career book. *Love Your Job!* . . . takes you on an exciting inner tour and helps you to map your heart, soul, and motivation so that in the end you learn who you are and what you truly love to do."

Dr. Stephen Bishop, President, Bishop Consulting Group

"This book is more than how to find a rewarding job. The techniques described and illustrated in work situations can be broadened to a whole philosophy of life."

Donna Weinberg, President, Weinberg & Associates

"A concise guide for anyone involved in today's unsettled job market . . . the networking information alone is worth the price of the book."

King Hughes, President, Ocean County Cellular

Love Your Job!

Loving the Job You Have...
Finding a Job You Love

Reflections, Stories, and Practical Exercises
for Good Times and Bad

By Dr. Paul Powers & Deborah Russell

O'Reilly & Associates, Inc.
103 Morris Street, Suite A
Sebastopol, CA 95472

Love Your Job!

by Dr. Paul Powers & Deborah Russell

Editor: Deborah Russell

Printing History:

August 1993:   First Edition.

1-56592-036-8   [10/93]

For Dr. Alan B. Sostek

Psychologist, mentor, colleague, friend

Our Thanks

Our special thanks to Tim O'Reilly, who believed in this book from the beginning and urged us to take a chance on making it a very different kind of book from the one we started with. His encouragement and practical suggestions contributed immeasurably to keeping us on track and making this book what it is. Thanks, too, to those who reviewed early drafts of the book: Christina F. O'Reilly for her insightful comments and suggestions for new material, Barry Coughlin, Frank Cullen, Kevin Harrington, King Hughes, Ilene Lang, Christine Melchior, Joan Stoia, and Donna Weinberg.

Thanks as well to the many people at O'Reilly & Associates who turned our book into a polished product—to Edie Freedman and Jennifer Niederst who designed the book cover and format, to Mike Sierra and Clairemarie Fisher O'Leary who produced the final text, to Leslie Chalmers for her sensitive reading of the manuscript, and to Jill Berlin, John Dockery, Brian Erwin, Linda Lamb, Linda Mui, and Peter Mui who helped us to see more clearly what our book really was all about. Thanks to all the other folks at both O'Reilly & Associates and Cambridge Computer Associates who encouraged and helped in practical ways during the writing of this book, including Bonnie Hyland who kept us in touch with each other even when one of us operated on Powers Standard Time.

Finally, thanks to our families—to Linda Powers and to Chan, Kristin, Sarah, and Alex Russell, who gave us encouragement and welcome distraction while we wrote this book—and who are the main reasons we love life outside, as well as inside, our jobs!

—Dr. Paul Powers & Deborah Russell

Table of Contents

Do You Love Your Job?

Do you love your job? I begin many of my seminars and workshops by asking that question. In fact, I ask it wherever I go—alumni events, professional meetings, parties, even shopping and waiting in lines for planes and buses. The answers I hear are pretty disheartening.

Do You Love Your Job?

Most People Don't

Pretty consistently, only about one person in ten answers "yes" to the question, "Do you love your job?" In *Working and Liking It,* Richard Germann, Diane Blumenson, and Peter Arnold report that four out of five workers dislike at least one major aspect of their jobs. In *Do What You Love, The Money Will Follow,* Marsha Sinetar puts the number at 95 percent.

I think these are horrible statistics. Most of us will work close to 100,000 hours during our lifetimes—about half the waking hours of our entire adult lives. When you consider that we invest so many hours—month after month, year after year—in our work, it's sad that this investment pays off so little in terms of personal satisfaction.

Do our feelings about our work really make a difference? Absolutely! If you don't love your job, you're going to feel it and show it. You may get your job done. But you're going to be bored, frustrated, angry, or apathetic. And those feelings will show up in both personal and professional ways.

Maybe you'll react by getting sick a lot. There is evidence that the stress and boredom you suffer at work—spinning your wheels, worrying about being fired, or biding your time until retirement—may damage your health. In a series of new studies, the International Labor Organization (ILO) found that 45 percent of salaried workers in the United States say they experience excessive stress, and 15 percent report depression. In another recent study, cardiologist Dr. Peter L. Schnall of New York Hospital in New York City found that people complaining of strain on the job were more likely to have high blood pressure, as well as thickening of the muscles on the walls of the heart— both risk factors for heart attacks. A seminal 1972 study conducted in Massachusetts showed that the surest predictor of heart disease was not smoking, cholesterol, or lack of exercise, but job dissatisfaction. Other more recent studies have linked job stress and dissatisfaction with the risk of developing ulcers, hypertension, and increased rates of insomnia, alcoholism, suicide, and even workplace violence.[1] (Witness the alarming series of fatal shootings at post offices and other workplaces in recent years.)

Maybe you'll do the minimum necessary at work and outside it. You probably won't take courses or attend seminars that might help you do your job better. Your relationship with your boss, your coworkers, and your subordinates will suffer.

Maybe you won't go the extra mile to try out new technologies, like computers, electronic mail, desktop publishing techniques, specialized auto repair tools or medical instruments—whatever is new in your own profession. Maybe you won't put in the extra effort to read the business pages or network among people who might help your company grow—or help you find something else to do.

This personal and professional slackening off is likely to keep you out of the inner circle of people who make a difference in your organization and in your profession. And then you'll *really* hate your job.

Look at the big picture. If an organization is full of people who don't like what they do, and who do the minimum necessary to keep their jobs, that organization is inevitably going to suffer. And think of the overall impact on our country's morale and economy if *every* company is full of such people. There are complaints these days that the work energy and ethic of America has already damaged our ability to compete in markets around the world.

Wow! Disease, disillusionment, and global economic collapse—all because you don't bounce out of bed happy every morning!

Have I exaggerated? Maybe a bit. Lots of people don't like their jobs, and nothing really bad happens to them or to their organizations. But nothing really good happens either. Think about your last unhappy experience with a government bureaucracy. Was it the Department of Motor Vehicles? The IRS? Your State Unemployment Office? There are many happy, productive government workers; don't get me wrong. But I'll bet even money that when you next dance "the bureaucratic shuffle," you'll look around and see a lot of unhappy faces. How do I know this? Because happy, challenged, productive employees don't give you the runaround. They act in an engaging, helpful, and friendly way.

Why Does It Matter?

Why do our jobs matter so much? Why do we *need* to love them? Is this business of loving our jobs just another symptom of the feel-good generation? Who promised us a rose garden, after all?

Some people think I'm dreaming the impossible dream when I talk about loving a job, especially in an economy in which so many people don't even *have* jobs. Many people don't think *anybody* can really love a job. "Hey, it's just a job," they tell me. A lot of our parents and friends say they've felt lucky to have any job at all. What does it matter? Work isn't all there is to life, is there? It's not everything, of course, but it's more important than most of us realize—in terms of commitment, personal connections, and self-worth.

Think about the time and energy you need to put into a job, even one you *don't* like, just to keep it. Wouldn't it be nice if you could treat that time and energy as an investment in your future and in your happiness, rather than as a waste of time and a drain of energy you'd rather be expending on something else? Most of us need to work—for money, of course, but also to give our lives a sense of structure and self-esteem. Wouldn't you like to get something back from your work—something beyond a regular paycheck?

We let our jobs define us—more than we should, perhaps, considering all the other things that are, or should be, important in our lives. Children are always asked, "What do you want to be when you grow up?" At parties, the first question we ask of each other is often, "What do you do?"—and we don't mean at home, on the beach, or with our children.

To help answer the question of why our jobs are so important, I sometimes ask the people who attend my workshops a different question: "How many of you know four or five people in your neighborhood or building really well?" Then I ask: "How many of you know four or five people you work with really well?" Overwhelmingly, very few people answer "I do" to the first question, but most do to the second.

I grew up in Milford, Massachusetts, in a community where everybody had lived for years and years. We all knew our neighbors, their kids, their problems, and their successes. In the town where I now live, I know one neighbor well, another fairly well, a few more by name, and the rest not at all.

For better or for worse, the workplace has become what I call "the new neighborhood." Work is where we show our vacation pictures, where we complain or boast about our spouse and our kids, where we reminisce about the past, and fantasize about the future. We spend far more time with our coworkers than we do with our neighbors. In fact, we spend more time with our coworkers than we do with the people we profess to love most in our lives—our families.

Statistics show that Americans are now working 15 percent longer hours than they did 20 years ago, although it's not clear that the increased hours actually result in increased productivity. With recessionary times, complaints about the American work ethic, and specters of ever-increasing global competition, that trend shows no indication of reversing itself. Much of the year, many of us leave home in the dark, and return in the dark. Our feeling of community—if it exists at all—has to be satisfied in the workplace.

I'm not going to tell you that this is how it should be. But, like it or not, this is how it is for many of us. And, because it is this way, because we spend the majority of our waking, most productive hours at work, it's all the more important that we feel happy and fulfilled doing that work. Becoming successful in that work—making sure that the time and energy and commitment we pour into our careers leads to some measurable progress in our lives—is more critically important to our generation than it has ever been before.

It's More than the Money

Some people who are unhappy in their work tell me they'd be happy—they'd *really* love their jobs—if they just made more money. Of course, we all need enough money to survive, support our families, and feel good about ourselves. But money alone won't turn the job you have into a job you'll love.

Even being born into a company with your name on it doesn't guarantee job satisfaction. Sons and daughters of company founders may rise quickly to the top of the heap, but the silver spoon doesn't guarantee that they'll like what they do—and it certainly won't guarantee that other people in the organization will like it either. The result can be personally and professional devastating. Think about Fred Wang, heir to Wang Laboratories, who rose to the presidency of the company without the experience, the support, and perhaps the personal fire to keep him there.

My own experience, working with people who are looking for jobs, leaving jobs, loving jobs, and hating jobs, has convinced me that money is not the key. Less tangible job characteristics—things like challenge, responsibility, the ethics of an organization, the ability to put your dreams into action, and that special fit between you and the job—these are the qualities that make you truly love a job.

What Makes a Job Lovable?

The reasons that one person loves her job, and another person hates his job, are very personal ones. These reasons often have to do more with the person's psychology than with the concrete facts of the job. Different people want and need different kinds and combinations of job satisfaction. They're picking from a huge variety of reasons and putting together an equation that's right—or not right—for them and them alone.

It's almost always a mistake to think that any single characteristic of a job is enough reason for a person—any person—to love that job. Usually, you have many very personal reasons for loving a job. A job you love is a good match between your own psychological makeup and specific needs with the particulars of what you do all day.

Too many of us are hung up on finding that one star, that one pot of gold. Some books talk about finding your "true life's work," or your "one right road." For some people, that's possible—the young girl who knows from her first glimpse of a bandaid that she wants to be a surgeon, or the small boy who sits down at the piano at age five and stays there until he's a concert pianist. For most of us, though, there is no single answer to the question: "What is the right career—or job—or life path—for me?"

Some people are so focused on finding the one right answer that they become immobilized. They're looking for the pot of gold at the end of the rainbow, the winning lottery ticket, the magic bullet. They won't experiment with learning new trades, or new fields, until they've settled on what's exactly right for them. They won't work hard to improve their enjoyment of, or their performance at, the jobs they already have. They don't try to mold the almost right into the really right. Somebody once said, "Perfection is just a succession of approximately rights." Sometimes, you've got to play around with "approximately right" until you've turned it into something that truly is just right for you.

For most of us there is no single shining star that we're destined to follow for our entire careers or lives. Most of us have a group of interests, a varied (and sometimes conflicting) set of personal characteristics, and a diverse set of work, avocational, and personal skills that all need to be factored into our decision about our life's work. Instead of searching for that solitary, shining star, I advise people to identify the top five or ten stars that form their own personal, motivational constellation:

Do you need a job that's always changing?

Do you want to feel that you're helping others through your work?

Do you need a lot of responsibility, or does that idea frighten you?

Do you want to be in the public eye, or is public visibility a big negative for you?

Do you have an eye for detail or do you have a good sense of the big picture?

Do you have a need for structure, or are you happier in an open and independent environment?

If you need structure, you might be miserable in a free-wheeling environment, with no formal management levels and no clear plan for responding to problems. If you like to think on your feet and make it up as you go along, this might be just the right place for you. There are all types of jobs and all types of people. Your challenge is to figure out what type of person you are before you plunge into somebody else's dream job.

The very best type of job lets you be yourself in the context of your work. In the simplest words, it makes you happy. In this book, I try my best to help you identify a job you'll love—as well as the qualities in yourself that will make you open to finding and keeping that job. But I want you to remember that there may be many right jobs for you, and that you might even be able to mold a job that isn't right into one that is.

Don't Settle for Second-Best

The main message of this book is simple: Don't settle for too little in your job. Your time at work isn't a dress rehearsal for something better. This is it—this is the only life you've been issued. Remember, you'll spend half the waking hours of your adult life at work! Don't waste any one of those hours.

Whoever you are, whatever your gifts, passions, and background, you have the capacity to find and keep a job you will love. You may have to struggle to find your way. You may need some additional training. You may not be able to shoehorn yourself into a traditional job or organization; instead, you may need to invent the job that truly suits you best. But, many, many other people have done it; you can too!

If you're an employer, encourage your employees to find ways to love their jobs too. Too many employers act as if the happiness of their employees is actually a threat to their business, rather than the wonderful boon that it can be. In fact, happy, motivated workers—people who are making their dreams come true—will do more for your business and for your own morale than the biggest new customer or the most effective cost cuts.

How important is work in our lives? In Working, *Studs Terkel says it best:*

> [Work is] about a search, too, for daily meaning as well as daily bread, for recognition as well as cash, for astonishment rather than torpor; in short, for a sort of life rather than a Monday through Friday sort of dying.

About This Book

During most of my years as a management psychologist, I've wanted to write a book that looked at the world of work from the perspective of a psychologist—someone who is concerned not only with helping people find jobs, but also helping them love those jobs and feel enriched, both financially and emotionally, by them. I've never been able to find the time to fulfill this goal. Finally, Deborah Russell, a friend who works as an acquisitions editor and author for O'Reilly & Associates (primarily a computer book publishing company) suggested that we work together to get my ideas down on paper. I'm afraid I did a lot more of the talking, and she did a lot more of the writing. But, in the end, this book is a true collaboration, not just an "as told to" kind of book. I think it has truly brought out the best in both of us.

The story didn't end with our collaboration. This book you're reading isn't the book we originally wrote. We wrote a book like many other books—organized into chapters and filled with practical advice about how to write a winning resumé, what to do in an interview, and how to negotiate for a job you love. When our publisher, Tim O'Reilly, read the draft, he said, "There's a lot of good, inspiring stuff in here, but it's buried." All the clear, specific advice we'd labored over wasn't really saying what we wanted said; the most important part of the book was obscured by the facts and figures.

The critical part of finding a job you love—whether it's in an office or out on the range, whether it's in a job that will require you to drop everything and go back to school or simply to look more clearly at the job you're already doing—is to understand yourself and what satisfies you. More than teaching you to write a stellar resumé or to put on a happy face for your 99th interview, we're urging you to open your mind to new work possibilities, and to look inside your heart for how you love to spend your time and energy.

So many books teach you the "how to" of career choice and job hunting. We want to focus on the "why," the very personal reasons why you should care about your job and who you can be in that job.

In the end, we decided to organize this book into a set of thoughts—call them reflections or executive summaries—that we hope will stimulate your own thinking about yourself, your dreams, and your career, along with a set of practical exercises to get you going on the path of finding and keeping a job you love. We've organized these reflections into four sections:

What Does It Mean to Love Your Job?

Can you really love a job? Isn't money what really matters? Surprisingly, what you earn at what you do isn't nearly as important as how you feel about what you do.

Can You Keep Loving Your Job?

The most lovable job won't remain lovable if it doesn't grow along with you. How can you keep improving your job so it keeps challenging you? How can you keep learning and growing and changing yourself so you keep offering more and more to your job?

What if You Don't Have a Job You Love?

You may find there's no way to turn the job you have into a job you love. Then, it's time to move on. You may have loved—and lost—your job. Or, you may be hunting for a job for the first time. What's next for you?

Is There Life Outside Your Job?

Even the most challenging and rewarding job isn't enough. How can you juggle all the demands of life inside and outside your job, and still find time for relaxation and even some fun?

We've included many stories of people we've worked with over the years—people who love their jobs, people who hate their jobs, and people who have learned to change their jobs and their careers and their minds—and have, in that way, changed their lives. Whip through these pages from start to finish, or open them at random whenever you're puzzled about why you're not happier about the way you're spending your days and your life.

All of the stories recounted in these pages are true. However, in most cases, we've changed the names and, in some cases, certain identifying characteristics, of the people whose stories we tell, to avoid any embarrassment to them, their families, or their organizations.

We include exercises in this book, not as a way of enforcing a rigid curriculum or a step-by-step, "Get a Job in 30 Days" type of approach, but as a way of stirring you to take some action. I find, in my work with people looking for jobs, as well as people looking for other sources of satisfaction in their lives, that those who ask questions and take action each step of the way are much more likely to change, grow, and prosper than those who read, ponder, and delay action until they've put together a fully coordinated plan. I hope the exercises will get you thinking and asking questions of yourself and others.

Ralph Waldo Emerson said, "By necessity, by proclivity—and by delight, we all quote." I find it thought-provoking to read the great words of others, and I hope that the quotations we've used to introduce most of the pages in this book will shed additional light on our own words. Emerson also said, "I hate quotations." I hope you don't agree!

I've loved working with the people whose stories fill these pages, and I've loved writing this book. My greatest hope is that in some way I can help you to love your work as much as I love mine.

—Dr. Paul Powers

What Does it Mean to
Love Your Job?

A job you love is a job that lets you act on your passions as well as your skills. The "right" job in some way, or some mix of ways, enlarges you. It improves the quality of your entire life, not just the part of your life you spend at work. In a very fundamental way, if you're happy at work, if you love your job, you're much more likely to be happy outside your work, to love your life as a whole.

On the other hand, a job that isn't right for you reduces in some way, or some mix of ways, the quality of your life. The jobs people hate—and these jobs may range from company president to trash collector, from fast food clerk to airline pilot—make them feel angry, resentful, and at some level betrayed. Feeling that you're giving of yourself without getting something equivalent in return drains your energy, saps your motivation, and generally makes you feel like a smaller person.

Ask the Question

To ask the hard question is simple.

W.H. Auden
Poems, Number 27

WHEREVER I GO, I ask the people I meet if they love their jobs. I ask everybody—executives, bellboys, bartenders, maids, firefighters. If they say yes, I ask them why. If they say no, I also ask them why.

What amazes me most is the large number of people who have never thought about the question. Do they love their jobs? They don't really know if they love—or even like—their jobs. Nobody has ever asked them before. And they haven't asked themselves.

So, ask yourself right now: Do you love your job? If you do, why? If you don't, why? What do you want out of your work? Out of your life? Are you getting the return you're entitled to?

Stirring things up in your mind is often the first step on the road to identifying and finding a job you'll love. Let your mind wander freely. Don't dismiss any idea:

- Even if the changes you'd need to make in your present job seem impossibly drastic.

- Even if the job you'd love seems completely out of reach.

- Even if you find that you need years of training for a new field.

- Even if you don't think you can afford to make a change—financially or emotionally.

Yes, even if. The very act of starting to picture yourself—in your own mind—as someone who is capable of achieving that job you could love—will give you some satisfaction. And that feeling of satisfaction will help you make progress towards your goal.

What do you really love? With sufficient drive and commitment, you can do just about anything you want to do. But if you can identify what really excites you in a profession, then instead of using your energy to push yourself in the wrong direction, you'll focus every bit of that energy on pulling you forward into a world that suits your personality, appreciates your commitment, and challenges your mind and heart. Imagine getting up every morning wanting to get to work to face what the day will bring. With energy and devotion like that, imagine how far you'll be able to go!

Dream a Big Dream

Le seul rêve intéresse.
What is life, without a dream?

Edmond Rostand
La Princesse Lointaine

MOST PEOPLE HAVE DREAMS, and jobs, too small for their spirits.
Small children talk confidently about becoming President and flying to the moon.
Children's dreams usually revolve around challenge, excitement, and even danger—
seldom around salary and a parking space. When do we start settling for far smaller
and more concrete accomplishments? Somebody actually does become President, fly
to the moon, write books, and move mountains—why not you? Why is it so hard for
us as adults to visualize a way of making a living that comes close to the exciting,
heroic possibilities we dreamed as kids?

An Exercise in Dreaming

1. Get yourself a notebook and, for at least a month, carry it with you wherever you go.

2. What is your dream? What do you fantasize about doing as work? Don't let yourself think, "I can't," "I don't know how," or "It's too late." You can worry about real-life problems and real-life constraints later on. For now, just dare to dream. Make a list of the first five dream jobs that come to mind. Would you love to run for office? Own your own bookstore? Buy a tractor/trailer and take to the road? Teach tennis to special needs children?

3. Throughout this month, whenever you see, hear, or think about something that fits into your dream, jot down your thoughts.

   Perhaps this will be a newspaper article about a firefighter who's just saved a life—or one about a romance novelist. Perhaps it will be a show by a radio DJ you admire. Perhaps it will be a memory of an experience you had in school—giving a fiery speech, doing a chemistry experiment that worked, or organizing a bake sale and presenting the proceeds to a homeless shelter. Perhaps it will be an insight that the volunteer work or pottery or writing you do could turn into a paying job. By the end of the month you should have a clearer mental image of a person, a type of person, or a set of activities that put your dream into somewhat more tangible terms.

Set the Bar High Enough

Ah, but a man's reach should exceed his grasp,
Or what's a heaven for?

Robert Browning
Andrea del Sarto

THE ONE OVERRIDING CHARACTERISTIC of successful people is that they set the bar high enough. What do I mean by this? In high-jumping, athletes compete by setting the bar at a certain height; then, if they successfully clear the bar at that height, they set it higher and still higher. Eventually, of course, they fail to clear the bar. But—and this is important—they're never able to beat an opponent, or set a new record, if the bar isn't set high enough to make failure a possibility.

In sports, athletes are always pushing the envelope, raising the bar, driving themselves a little harder to reach a goal that only months or even weeks ago might have seemed unattainable. But so few people in "regular life" treat their careers with the same verve. Few of us dream big enough dreams, and push hard enough to achieve them.

People who really love their jobs set the bar high enough. Lower would assure a passing grade, a minimal promotion, a small pat on the back. Higher might risk a reprimand, a losing ad campaign, a company reorganization that didn't live up to expectations. But higher might also mean a big triumph and an unforgettable feeling of achievement. Successful people think carefully before picking the height of the bar—but once it's set, they go for it with all they've got.

Listen to Your Own Voice

Just as the twig is bent, the tree's inclined.

Alexander Pope
Moral Essays, Epistle I

POPE WASN'T ALWAYS RIGHT. We are all capable of outstripping early expectations, tapping hidden potential, and growing beyond the fate predicted for us.

I love reading biographies, and I've been amazed at how many of my heroes got less than rave reviews when they were children. Listen to these comments about children who thankfully listened to their own voices and dreamed their own dreams, rather than those of their teachers:

> *I am very concerned about her. She is bright and full of curiosity, but her interest in bugs and other crawling things, and her daredevil projects, are just not fitting for a young lady.* (about Amelia Earhart)

> *He is a unique member of the class. He is ten years old and only beginning to read and write. He is showing signs of improving, but you must not set your sights too high for him.* (about Woodrow Wilson)

> *He is a very poor student. He is mentally slow, unsociable, and is always daydreaming. He is spoiling it for the rest of the class. It would be in the best interests of all if he were removed from school at once.* (about Albert Einstein)

And remember too that Enrico Caruso's teacher declared him to have "no voice," that Louisa May Alcott's first editor swore that "she would never write anything for popular consumption," that Admiral Byrd was retired from the Navy because he was "unfit for service," and that Billy Mitchell was court-martialed for suggesting that the era of battleships was over and the future of our country's defense was in airplanes.

There are some wonderful counter-examples too. Pediatrician and author T. Berry Brazelton tells how his grandmother inspired his career by telling him, and others, throughout his childhood, "Berry is so good with children." Brazelton came to believe in his own competence. His long and successful career, ministering to children and their parents, was nurtured by that wonderful combination of initial interest and positive reinforcement from the world around him.

If you believe you can do something, go for it! Don't let other people—teachers, parents, employers, or friends—limit your dreams.

Do You Do It For the Money?

And no one shall work for money,
and no one shall work for fame,
But each for the joy of the working,
and each, in his separate star,
Shall draw the Thing as he sees
It for the God of Things as They are!

Rudyard Kipling
The Seven Seas, "When Earth's Last Picture Is Painted"

WHAT MOTIVATES YOU to work hard? What makes you love your job? Is it money?

Psychologist Frederick Herzberg has conducted numerous studies of motivation in the workplace. In *Work and the Nature of Man* and other books and articles, Herzberg reports on the results of interviews of workers in countries as widespread as the United States, Hungary, Finland, and the former Soviet Union, and groups as diverse as senior managers, manufacturing assemblers, low-level supervisors, agricultural administrators, hospital janitors, food handlers, nurses, military officers, engineers, scientists, housekeepers, teachers, technicians, and accountants. He has found that money, along with other concrete job characteristics, does not motivate us to work harder and enjoy our jobs.[2]

Herzberg distinguishes between *hygiene factors*—salary, working conditions, status, job security, and level of supervision, and *motivators*—achievement, recognition, responsibility, the work itself, and growth or advancement in your job. The factors leading to job satisfaction (motivators) are quite separate from the factors leading to job dissatisfaction (hygiene factors).

If you don't make enough money and you hate your working conditions, you'll be dissatisfied with your job. But the opposite doesn't hold true. If you do make enough money, you won't necessarily be satisfied with your job—or motivated to do it better.

In *Divorcing a Corporation*, Jacqueline Hornor Plumez takes it a step further. She calls money, and other tangible assets of a job, "golden handcuffs" because they may lock us into jobs that are wrong for us. Her book provides another slant on the reasons why people enjoy, or stay with, their jobs.[3]

What Keeps You from Hating Your Job?

Here are some of the concrete reasons people have given me for why they don't hate their jobs.

- I make as much money as I deserve (well, almost).
- If I keep doing my job well, I'll have a good chance of more income in the future (through salary increases, stock, profit-sharing, and retirement/pension programs).
- I get acceptable benefits (insurance, vacation).
- The perks (a car, a parking space, tuition reimbursement) are OK.
- I like the location (safe neighborhood, good commute, near family, friends, activities).
- I have the latest and best equipment, tools, and supplies.
- The working conditions (my own office, a kitchen, clean rest rooms) are OK.
- I like the amount of travel I need to do.
- My boss is a reasonable person to work for.
- I don't have any problems with company policy.
- I get along well with my coworkers.

If It's Not Money, What Is It?

For I don't care too much for money,
Money can't buy me love.

John Lennon and Paul McCartney
Can't Buy Me Love

MONEY DOESN'T MAKE US love our jobs or motivate us to do better at them. It just keeps us from hating them. What are the qualities of a job that make us truly love that job?

Frederick Herzberg finds that those qualities are usually more related to intangible factors, like growth on the job, responsibility, and challenge, than to the specifics of money and status.

Jobs we love demand much of us—not only our time, but our devotion. They challenge us to do more and better every day. They're dynamic, and they fit our own special profile of what's important to us. Herzberg puts it like this: "To feel that one has grown depends on achievement in tasks that have meaning to the individual."

For another look at the most basic reasons we love our jobs, consider discovering your "career anchors" through the techniques developed by Edgar H. Schein.[4] He writes:

> *Your career anchor is a combination of perceived ideas of competence,*
> *motives, and values that you would not give up; it represents your real self.*
> *Without knowledge of your anchor, outside incentives might tempt you into*
> *situations or jobs that subsequently are not as satisfactory because you feel*
> *that "this is not really me."*

What Makes You Love Your Job?

Here are some of the less concrete, and more individual, reasons people have given me for loving their jobs:

- The job challenges me in just the right way.
- I have the right amount of autonomy, responsibility, and independence in decision-making.
- My job has developed along with me.
- There are lots of opportunities for me to develop something of my own.
- I have some power within the organization (my ideas can result in policy changes).
- My family feels positive about my work here. (I don't work for the Mob.)
- I feel a sense of achievement and personal pride here.
- Senior management recognizes and appreciates my achievements.
- I can express my creativity.
- I like the pace (I like it frantic) (or, I like it mellow).
- My job is in some way a useful one. (Socially, I'm a part of the solution, not a part of the problem.)
- I'm learning new skills and getting valuable experience.
- My job doesn't demand that I act like someone I'm not.
- It's work I inherently enjoy (e.g., I like to write, and that's what the job entails).
- The job is fun—I look forward to doing it just about every day!

Don't Settle for Money Alone

That's where the money is.

Willie Sutton, in response to the question,
"Why do you rob banks?"

ALTHOUGH MOST OF US say the best things in life are free, too many of us are willing to settle for a trailer load of second best.

I think if you work at a job just for the money—and you have a choice in the matter—then you, like Willie Sutton, are a robber. You're stealing from yourself the opportunity to do something that uses more of your talents and skills, something that recharges you instead of leaving you drained. You're probably also robbing your employer, who could find somebody to do your job better—and to love it too.

Ted Burns, a lawyer at a large Boston law firm, is unhappy with his work but is completely unwilling to think about leaving the firm. "The only reason I'm here is the money," he says, "but it's the only way I know to make the money I make." He has a large family, a large house, a pool, and college tuitions. I tell him that he could practice law in a more congenial environment—perhaps a college or a social service agency or even a movie studio. I believe his legal training would be applicable in many other fields too—as a teacher, a lobbyist, or a writer. He might make less money, it's true, but his family could survive and his happiness would be so much greater. But Ted won't even let himself explore. He's locked into his life style and his image of himself as a rich, successful lawyer. He's stealing from himself a shot at a happier and more fulfilling life.

90% Is Pretty Close

Nothing is perfect. There are lumps in it.

James Stephens
The Crock of Gold

A JOB YOU LOVE may not be a perfect job. Every job has its deficiencies, its boring moments, its lumps. You've got to know what to ignore. A surgeon who loves the thrill of using hard-earned talents to save lives may hate the dreariness of having to worry about billing and office management. Do insurance regulations negate the satisfaction of surgery? Not for most doctors. A park ranger may love working in the beauty of a national park but may hate dealing with careless campers who leave debris and sometimes even fire behind. A scientist may love research but hate writing reports and grant proposals.

There are pros and cons to any job. A job you love is a job that has many more pros than cons—as well as an overriding rightness to it. Chuck Nelson teaches history and social studies to junior high school students. His job has a number of negatives. It pays poorly relative to what his friends in the business world are earning. Teaching junior high school students, with their high energy, peer group issues, and frequent defiance of authority, is often exhausting. Even more exhausting, and sometimes frustrating, are his administrative duties. And Chuck finds it difficult at times being one of only a few men teaching at his school. But, despite the negatives, Chuck can't imagine doing anything but teaching. "That moment when I really engage their minds in the classroom—when they light up because I'm getting through, and they're caring about what they're learning," he says, "I don't think anything can compare to it."

What Type of Work Is Right for You?

Blessed is he who has found his work;
let him ask no other blessedness.

Thomas Carlyle
Past and Present

FINDING A JOB YOU LOVE means finding just the right match between a real-life situation and your dreams, skills, and personal qualities. Not every "right" job needs to offer romance and adventure. Some people love menial jobs that you might expect them to hate. Others land their dream jobs and find them a nightmare.

I once worked as a consultant at an international bank in New York City. In the bank's 200-person regional bank data processing center, I met Joan Howard. Joan was responsible for what was called Error Identification and Reconciliation. She worked in a 6' × 6' cubicle surrounded by stacks of computer printouts that threatened to topple, at any moment, and bury her alive. Joan was the person responsible for examining printouts, line by line, using a special plastic ruler, identifying coding errors, looking up the proper codes in her computer database, and entering them—either by marking the correct code by pen on the printout or by typing the code on her computer terminal. To me, it was a nightmare of a job: slow, tedious, and lonely. But Joan *loved* it.

Years before, Joan told me, she started in the bank as a teller and was promoted to Customer Service. She disliked dealing with the public in a fast-paced branch office, surrounded by windows on two sides and cameras on the other two. She tried to quit, but her boss persuaded her to work with the bank's Human Resources department. After formal assessment of Joan's interests and personality, Human Resources helped pinpoint the job in which Joan thrived.

Sadly, most companies don't try very hard to help employees find the best places for them in an organization. So, it's going to be up to you to figure out where you belong—in your own organization or another one.

An Exercise in Job Matching

1. When you daydream about being successful in your job, what does your dream look like? Where are you physically? Indoors or outdoors? A hospital? A boardroom? A courtroom? A tennis court?

2. Who is with you? A boss? A small group of coworkers? An audience? Nobody?

3. What tools are you using? A computer? A violin? A spade? A hammer? Are you driving a truck? The space shuttle? A school bus?

4. Who have you met or seen who you admire? This might be a person you know well, someone you've just met, or someone you've seen only on the news. It might even be a character in a movie or a novel. Is it a former boss? A speaker at a conference you've attended? A political figure?

5. What activities does this person perform that makes them seem admirable? Do they have material success? Interesting or dangerous or crowd-pleasing work? A loving family? Dedication to society?

Learn From Your Failures

There is the greatest practical benefit in making a few failures early in life.

Thomas Henry Huxley
On Medical Education

I THINK A GOOD DEFINITION of success is "learning from your failures." We all fail sometimes, at something. Your failures provide you with invaluable information. There's no better place to learn what you can do—and what you can't do or don't want to do.

Often, when you're not doing well at something, you blame yourself—and others may blame you too. It's entirely possible, though, that you are working hard—but at the wrong thing. We're not all good at everything. The square peg in the round hole isn't a misshapen round peg. It just needs a new home.

There are many different kinds of gifts and types of intelligence. Straight As in high school may demonstrate only that you can get straight As in high school. Some very successful people were mediocre students, had lackluster early careers, and were fired from several jobs. How did they finally make it? They didn't suddenly get smart. They simply found what was right for them.

I studied biology in high school under the tutelage of Sister Ronald, who wouldn't let us use the laboratory equipment because we might break it or get it dirty. I'm a hands-on type person, and the abstraction of studying experiments, instead of doing them, was not up my alley. Sister Ronald told my father that, in addition to failing the course, I'd probably fail life. Imagine her surprise when I managed to get a Ph.D. But notice that the degree was in psychology, *not* biology. The peg found its rightful hole.

Try not to view failure as a complete negative. If you're not punished unduly for your unsuccessful attempts, you may find that "failing" is the best possible way to learn. Gymnasts and figure skaters fall over and over again in the early stages of learning a new move. Have they failed each time? No. Each time they fall, they learn a little more about how to stand up next time.

An Exercise in Studying Your Failures

Do you feel like a failure? Ask yourself:

1. What type of industry are you in? Do you feel as if you belong there? If you feel adrift in high-tech, is it possible that you belong in education, finance, or rodeo instead?

2. What type of organization are you in? Do you feel comfortable? Do you wish your company were more structured? More informal? Bigger? Smaller?

3. What type of function are you performing? Is it possible that you should be in sales instead of accounting? Research instead of sales? Maintenance instead of administration? Management instead of customer service?

4. Do you honestly feel that you'd be a failure anywhere, or do you think that you just don't fit in where you are?

Learn from Your Successes, Too

Rien ne réussit comme le succès.
Nothing succeeds like success.

French Proverb

WHAT ARE YOU GOOD AT? Think about your successes in the same analytical way you studied your failures. Don't just look at your skills—tangible things like whether you did well in accounting jobs or sales jobs or child care jobs. Try to go beyond the job titles to the underlying characteristics and feelings of those jobs.

Don't stop with your work life. Look critically at whatever you've made a success of—a sport, a hobby, an aspect of your home life. Let your success in one area of life guide you to other areas too.

Sometimes, when successful people turn to endeavors outside the workplace, the work ethic and habits of mind that have made them successful at work make them successful outside of it as well. Dr. W. Edwards Deming, the quality control specialist whose ideas about quality development and management brought him special renown in Japan, is also a talented composer who has published sacred music. Actor Anthony Quinn is also a talented and productive painter. Vincent Price is a gourmet cook and the author of several cookbooks.

If you've worked hard enough to do something really well, something that sets you apart, you may decide to try to make a career out of that achievement. You may also find that by applying the same enthusiasm and dogged determination to another arena, you'll make another, very different success.

An Exercise in Studying Your Successes

Think about your most successful experiences in the past—at work, in a sport, a hobby, a social setting? What were the two or three best days you've ever had? What made these peak experiences so satisfying?

1. Can you characterize the type of work you were doing when you felt successful? Did you save a life? Did you make a deal that brought you financial rewards? Did you overcome odds? Did you find a shortcut that helped you be more productive? Did you feel a closeness to your coworkers? To a class? To an audience?

2. Were you working with your hands? With numbers? With words? With abstract concepts? With people?

3. Were you working with a large group? With a few other people? Alone? With adults? With children? With people who were dependent on you (hospital patients, therapy clients)? With people in senior positions (CEOs, doctors, law partners)? With people similar to you in background and training? With people different from you?

4. Were you helping these people? Selling to them? Negotiating with them? Fighting them?

5. Was your triumph a lucky break or the result of work over a long period of time?

6. How might you be able to apply these past successes to your new career, job, or project? Open your mind. If you've loved writing for a small newspaper, you might also love writing grant proposals for a biotechnology company. If you've been happy running a day care center, maybe social work would appeal to you. If you feel comfortable selling a product, maybe you'd also enjoy doing public relations for a political candidate.

An Exercise in Looking at
Others' Successes

1. Explore your network of relatives, friends, and business contacts, and identify at least one or two people who make a living, or part of it, doing something that you've defined as a success.

   This might be a doctor. It might be someone who has written a book. It might be someone who does a dangerous, odds-defying sport. Don't worry about the person's particular job or profession. The key is to find someone who does some activity you've dreamed of doing, even if that person does it recreationally (for example, playing rugby, taking ballet or swimming lessons at the age of 40), or only occasionally in their work (for example, giving speeches, pulling off tough negotiations).

2. Contact each of these people. Tell them a little about yourself, and ask them to think back to the early stages of their own careers. What were they doing then that got them to where they are today? Use their responses to help think about what you might do to realize your own dream of success.

Keep Preparing for Success

The more I practice, the luckier I get.

Jack Nicklaus

THE MEDIA MAY LEAD you to believe that success strikes like lightning. One day you're poor, the next you're rich. One day you're a bum, the next a star. Luck has much to do with it, hard work very little.

Whenever a first-time novelist strikes it rich with a best-seller, a lot of media attention results, and would-be authors everywhere tell themselves, "That could have been me." It almost always turns out that, although this is the writer's first published work, several other novels languish, spurned and unpublished, in a drawer at home. The writer has practiced his or her craft long and hard before finally getting published.

"Overnight success" is very rare. A "sudden breakthrough" is almost always the culmination of years of practice, writing, or working—sometimes in solitude, sometimes in small companies or clubs or orchestras. During those years of trying and not quite succeeding, it's often hard to measure progress. The tenth song might be much better than the fifth, which is immeasurably better than the first, but when not one of them reaches the public, it's hard for the songwriter to declare himself a success. If you're able to appreciate the process that you're undertaking, and to notice the small successes along the way, you'll know that you've truly chosen the right work for you.

Marie Curie put it this way: "I was taught that the way of progress was neither swift nor easy."

Some years ago, I was chair of the Massachusetts Psychology Board. In my capacity, I met a former minister who had obtained his Ph.D. in psychology and was trying to pass the boards in order to practice. He had done well in his doctoral program, but he didn't test well, and time after time he failed the boards. But he kept plugging away, enjoying the work he did and continuing to believe in himself. Finally, during my last year as chair he passed on the sixth try. His progress was certainly not "swift and easy," but how he savored that eventual victory!

There Are Many Types of Success

By different methods different men excel.

Charles Churchill
An Epistle to William Hogarth

A LOT OF US SEEM to believe that success is only for successful people—the kinds of people you see in *People Magazine*. But anyone can be successful. In fact, some notoriously ordinary people have shed their C averages and their early boring jobs to make a lot of money, do a lot of good, and have a lot of fun with their careers. Why not you?

Dreams of success don't always involve running conglomerates and making millions. But they do involve using your talents to the utmost and making you feel happy and fulfilled. Not everybody is fodder for the talk shows. But all of us can be the best we can be in whatever walk of life we've decided is ours.

Frank Mirkin was an accounts receivable clerk who had a mediocre educational background, but a big dream of running his own business. People told him he ought to go back to school and become an accountant, but that traditional approach didn't appeal to him. One April, he did a coworker a favor by helping him do his taxes. The next year, several people offered to pay him for his help. He really enjoyed his tax work. What he particularly liked was not the accounting part of it, but finding ways that his clients could reduce their taxes in future years—by buying a house, opening an IRA, starting a small business, etc. Instead of taking the traditional route of accounting, he went back to school to become a certified financial planner, and eventually he set up a small practice, doing the kind of work he loves.

"Success" is a relative term. You'll need to decide what your own aspirations are, and how best to fulfill them in the context of your life—both inside and outside your job. Your own dreams of success might not mean life-and-death decisions, or constant vertical progress up the organizational chart. But, as long as you're working consistently and energetically towards a goal that's meaningful for you, you'll be a great success in the ways that count.

Do You Fear Success?

The danger chiefly lies in acting well;
No crime's so great as daring to excel.

Charles Churchill
An Epistle to William Hogarth

SURPRISINGLY, many people feel uneasy when things are going "too well"—when they get close to the goals they say they want to achieve. I'm sure you know people who have become self-destructive or dropped out of school in their senior years. I know a dozen or so people who have been declared "ABD" (All But Dissertation); they have completed all the coursework required for their Ph.D.'s, but they've run into roadblocks that have kept them from finishing their doctoral dissertations.

An expectedly large number of people fear success. Why should they? Some feel unworthy of success. Some fear the negative repercussions from that success. Some of us may have learned when we were young not to risk the wrath of our parents by proving them wrong or by surpassing their own achievements. Some have accepted the Calvinist message that pleasure—even the pleasure we find in our work—is sinful, and that we should take little personal credit for, or enjoyment of, our success.

How do we avoid success? Some people give up or develop psychosomatic illnesses; they just never try their utmost. Others become perfectionists, full of worry and anxiety about their progress. Others procrastinate, avoiding competition that might bring about success—maybe by finishing their papers or reports at the last minute so they can't do a really good job.

Think about Gary Hart. The Democratic front-runner in the 1988 quest for nomination, Hart foundered when the press sniffed out rumors of his extramarital affairs. "Follow me!" he challenged them. "I dare you to find something out." Follow him they did, straight to the townhouse of a woman—not his wife—with whom he apparently spent the night. The press and the American people were aghast, less at the situation's morality than at Hart's apparent stupidity. I think Hart was, at some level, afraid of success. He was getting too close to the prize; nobody else was wrecking his chances, so he had to blow it himself.

Not too many of us give up completely on success. The striving, achieving part of us keeps right on plugging away and trying to succeed. But for quite a few of us, there's a little voice inside telling us that we don't *really* want to make it. You'll need to understand why you feel the way you do before you can say no to that voice.

Overcome Your Fear of Success

*There are two tragedies in life. One is not to get
your heart's desire. The other is to get it.*

George Bernard Shaw
Man and Superman

MARTHA FRIEDMAN, in *Overcoming the Fear of Success*,[5] explores the reasons why people unconsciously fear success and may sabotage their behavior at work or at home to avoid reaching what they say are their life-long goals. She says the roots are almost always in early childhood experiences:

> *If certain factors have been operating in your psyche, factors that were incorporated in early childhood, you may well be living with a fear of success—even though to you the thought may appear to be completely aberrant. . . . The fear of success seems a paradox. On a conscious level, no one is afraid of success; everyone wants to be successful. But on an unconscious level, in that place few of us ever really explore, it's often quite a different story. There, in the unconscious, is where many of us do our best, without realizing it, to ensure that success is never reached or, if it is, that it doesn't last.*

Some people fear business success, others personal success. Some fear both, or the combination. A client of mine, Larry Romberg, was an international vice-president of sales who virtually abandoned his role as husband and father. He told me, "My father told me I would eventually have to choose—the way he had chosen—between having a happy home life and a successful business career." Deep down, Larry's father didn't *want* his son to surpass his own performance by balancing job and home life. And Larry was doing everything in his power to satisfy his father. At some level, he feared success in his home life because it would prove his father wrong.

It took time and energy, but once Larry recognized the roots of his behavior—how he was unconsciously sabotaging his own chances of making a success both at work and at home—he was able to make some changes and bring his life into better balance.

An Exercise in Confronting
Your Fear of Success

In *Overcoming the Fear of Success*, Dr. Friedman asks readers a long series of questions to detect what she calls "fear-of-success symptoms." If you answer yes to more than a few of these questions, many of which are excerpted from the book, with the permission of the author, I urge you to follow her advice on how you can overcome your own roadblocks to success.

1. Do you feel uneasy when things are going well?
2. Do you feel, deep down, that you may be a fraud?
3. Do you feel that if people really knew you, they wouldn't like you?
4. Does feeling good feel strange to you?
5. Does feeling bad feel good to you?
6. When you reach a goal you've been striving for, do you ask, "Is that all there is?"
7. Are you a workaholic?
8. Are you "a jack of all trades, but a master of none?"
9. Do you feel that competition is the root of all evil?
10. Would you rather be well-liked than competent?
11. Do weekends and free time make you anxious?
12. When you get something you want, do you find you don't want it anymore?
13. Are you a perfectionist?
14. Are you late no matter how hard you try to be on time?
15. Do you feel that good feelings can't last?
16. When something goes wrong, do you feel somehow responsible, even when you know you're not?

You Can Change

Change is not made without inconvenience,
even from worse to better.

Richard Hooker, quoted by Samuel Johnson

COULD THINGS BE BETTER at work? Can you make changes in the job you have now? Do you think you might love a different job, but you're worried that going out and changing jobs or even careers will disrupt your life? Are you saying to yourself, "My life is OK: not terrific, but not terrible either?" Are you asking, "What if things get worse instead of better?"

It would be strange if you weren't thinking these things. It's a completely normal human reaction to fear change. What can you do about it—besides curl up in a ball and keep everything just the same?

Try to think analytically about the other times in your life that you made changes. Maybe you got fired. Maybe you took a chance on a new career. Maybe you moved to a new part of the country. Maybe you changed schools. Maybe you married or divorced. Maybe you had a child, or said goodbye to a child who went off to college. Maybe you bought a house or made a risky investment. What were you afraid would happen as a result of these changes?

Mark Twain said: "I've known a lot of troubles in my time—and most of them never happened."

Some of the troubles we anticipate do come to pass. But most don't. There is often a lot more activity—certainly a lot more negative activity—in our heads than in our day-to-day lives.

An Exercise in Accepting Change

1. Think about the major changes you've faced before in your life.

2. Before each change took place, think of the four or five (or more) negative things you thought would happen as a result of the change. Here's an example:

   How about the time you went back to school nights to get your degree while you worked days. You feared:

   > "I'll be the oldest person in the class."

   > "I'll be totally out of touch with the other students and their concerns."

   > "I won't be able to keep up academically."

   > "I'll be too tired from studying to do well at work."

3. How many of these negative things actually happened?

   > "I was the oldest in the class—by far."

4. Of these, how many turned out as negatively as you thought they might? In our example, age actually worked to this student's advantage.

   > "As it turns out, the other students accepted me really well. In fact, I became sort of a mother figure to them. They told me their problems, and I did what I could to help. I really enjoyed getting to know them."

   Life sometimes takes unexpected turns.

Have the Courage to Find Your Own Path

Courage is the price that Life exacts for granting peace.

Amelia Earhart
Courage

MY EXPERIENCES in the military and in the occupational trenches have persuaded me that there are two distinct types of courage. One is the John Wayne type of courage—blast your way into the occupied village or the Western saloon and do what needs to be done (usually violently). The other is the courage to keep going faithfully on the path you've decided is the right one—even if the people around you disapprove or doubt. "If you can trust yourself when all men doubt you," as Kipling puts it, that's courage too.

People who have chosen a job they love—perhaps against others' opinions—are courageous, and their reward is a certain peace of mind. The work itself may be busy, even frantic. There may be financial stresses. But when you work at something you love, you aren't doubting yourself and your choice anymore, and that lifts a huge burden from you. Even if you don't make a success of your work, you'll have the great satisfaction of knowing that you tried your best to do what was best for you.

I worked with a young man, Clark Arnovitz, who graduated at the top of his business school class and went on to work at a successful high-tech company, rising to the job of aide-de-camp to the president. He liked his job, which was a hectic one, trying to keep up with the demands of a sometimes irascible boss and the daily turmoil of a growing company. But he didn't love the job. When a tragic accident took the life of the president, Clark took time out to think seriously about his own life and where he wanted it to lead him.

During his Boy Scout days, Clark had learned about beekeeping, and he'd kept up the hobby as an adult. When he thought long and hard about how he wanted to spend the rest of his life, it was bees, rather than computers, that buzzed the loudest. He got a lot of grief when he talked about his plans with his professional colleagues and professors. They thought he was throwing away a successful and still-developing career. Clark doubted himself at times, but he persisted. It took courage for him to continue on his chosen path. But he did it, and he's making a moderate success of his new career. There's been a lot of recent news about the benefits of eating honey—as relief for allergies, arthritis, and more—and Clark has benefited from the publicity. He now sells gourmet honey and is thoroughly happy that he exchanged his Brooks Brothers suits for farmer overalls.

Imagine!

Imagination is more important than knowledge.

Albert Einstein

EASY FOR HIM TO SAY! Einstein had more knowledge in his little finger than most of us have been able to pack into all our brain cells. It's significant, though, that one of the most profound thinkers of recent generations took time out from science and fact to emphasize the importance of imagination.

When I talk about imagination, I'm not necessarily focusing on the art of creating—music, painting, drama, etc. Anybody can imagine anything! And one of the most important things you can imagine is yourself—yourself in a wildly successful and satisfying future.

I'm not a mindless, rosy-eyed optimist who promises, "If you can see it, you can be it." Real-life issues and limitations sometimes stand in the way of our dreams. Rent, utilities, and car expenses often influence the direction our imaginings take. And our own limits can't always be denied. If you look like Frank Perdue, you're unlikely to be cast as a Mel Gibson type in the movies. It you're in a wheelchair, dancing in a Janet Jackson video is probably not on your horizon.

But don't give up completely on your wildest imaginings. So what if you don't look like Mel Gibson. Neither does Joe Pesci or Danny DeVito. There are plenty of terrific "character" roles—in the movies and in real life. So you'll be seeing life from a wheelchair. If you can't be a dancer, think about being a musician, a director, a production specialist.

Yakov Smirnoff came to America with a strong Russian accent and a memory of how hard things had been for him back home. He imagined himself successful, and parlayed the only things he had going for him into a successful career as a comedian. Victor Borge escaped the Nazis, leaving his career as a cabaret musician behind. In his new country, there was little interest in the kind of music that Borge had practiced in Europe, but the "King of Musical Madness" figured out how to combine his background and his sense of humor into a unique act that nobody has been able to equal.

Unleash your imagination. And remember, the only one holding the leash is you.

What's the Big Idea?

*There is one thing stronger than all the armies in the world;
and that is an idea whose time has come.*

Anonymous

WHY DID YOU BUY THIS BOOK? Was it simple curiosity? A clear belief that you needed to make a change in your work or in your life—by changing jobs or going back to school or starting a business of your own? Or was it a much vaguer feeling that things just weren't as good as they could be?

Sometimes, we're so busy with the day-to-day struggle to do our jobs and live our lives that we don't even let ourselves think about whether we're unhappy or dissatisfied or bored. But every once in a while, a fleeting idea will surface, a small message that things could be better. Somebody or something will catch our attention. Maybe it's the title of this book. Maybe it's a person we meet who seems to be living life to the fullest. Maybe it's a bad experience in the job we're doing now. The vague, gnawing feelings inside us start to coalesce.

At one time I worked in the executive search business. I didn't hate my work, but I didn't love it either. After I suffered through my thirty-sixth birthday, I started feeling old and anxious about what the rest of my life would bring. One day, I made what I thought was a clever pun, and my boss didn't get it. This does not rank with the world's worst offenses, but I said to myself, "I'm working for somebody who doesn't even appreciate my humor, never mind my work! Why?" From then on, there was no turning back. I'd crossed some threshold and somehow, without realizing it, had made my choice. From then on, I never had a doubt that I wanted to go into business for myself.

My reasons may sound flimsy, but the minor irritation that set me off was really the tip of the iceberg. Somehow, it crystallized the vague feelings I'd been experiencing but not really noticing.

Another pivotal moment in my work history came at a time when I'd been working with veterans in the psychiatric ward of a large hospital. We wore white coats (with name plates) in the hospital and usually left them there overnight. One day I discovered that one of my favorite patients had absconded with my coat and had been circulating around the hospital—visiting, diagnosing, and counseling patients—apparently with no adverse results. I was forced to ask myself only half in jest, "How good a job can I be doing if a patient can do it just as well?"

An Exercise in Turning Irritants to Concrete Questions

1. Think about what you'd like to change about your work life. Is there one basic problem you can identify and possibly change? Or are there many minor problems? Do you think you can work on making these changes while keeping your job, or do you need to make a fresh start?

2. Look back at your previous history. Who was the worst boss you've ever had? What were the qualities that you found particularly objectionable in Mr. or Ms. Crank? Note them and remember them. You never want to work for a person like this again.

3. Look back and think now about the worst environment you've ever worked in. What made it so bad? Were people unfriendly? Was the physical plant dirty, crowded, or uncomfortable in some other way? Was the company culture too formal or too informal for you? Did the company do something you found objectionable—make nerve gas, cheat the government, discriminate? Note these qualities and remember them. You never want to work in an environment like this again.

4. Look back and think now about the worst job function you've ever performed. What made it so bad? Was it physically frightening or uncomfortable (working with a jackhammer or radiation or small, unruly children)? Was it boring (endless filing or repetitive assembly line operations, or adding up numbers by hand)? Was it too demanding (trying to translate from a language you hadn't learned or sell a product you didn't understand)? Note these characteristics and remember them. You never want to perform a function like this again.

5. Do you have a nagging feeling that you ought to be doing something else? No matter how vague or unrealistic these feelings are, jot them down and look at them objectively, at least as an exercise. What is it you might want to do? What, realistically, is stopping you from doing it? If there is a path to the new job or career you've identified, what do you need to do to get started on that path?

6. Let these feelings jell for a while.

7. After a few weeks, go back to this exercise. See if your feelings about your current job or career are any clearer. Is it time to start thinking more concretely about taking that next step?

Put Your Passions
to Work for You

People don't choose their careers;
they are engulfed by them.

John Dos Passos
New York Times, October 25, 1959

MOST OF US CAN'T even imagine how much happier we might be working at something we truly love. Some of us stumble into jobs that really impassion us. But most of us have to work hard to figure out how to turn our passions into paying jobs.

A young man I know, Jason Beakin, was mired in a department of accountants on an entire floor of accountants at a large insurance company in Hartford, Connecticut. On an extended visit to California, where his sister lived, Jason was introduced to Californian and Mexican culture, and he took to it like the proverbial duck to water—the food, the drinks, the music, the laid-back ambiance. Jason was engulfed and enthralled.

Jason's roots were still in New England, but he couldn't imagine leaving the culture he'd learned to love. When he returned home, he started at once to figure out how he could make a living from his new passion. After a good deal of soul-searching and struggle, Jason started a Mexican restaurant. His strong business and financial skills, coupled with his complete conviction that he was doing what was right for him, made the venture a success.

Did he make millions? No. In his best years, the restaurant cleared only slightly more than Jason's accounting salary had been—and he worked twice as many hours! But Jason was able to give his sister and his elderly father jobs at Caramba; he got his fill of enchiladas, margaritas, and mariachi music; and he finally knew the rewards of making a living from passion, not obligation.

Never Stop Striving

*It is good to have an end to journey towards, but it is
the journey that matters in the end.*

Ursula K. Le Guin
The Left Hand of Darkness

A SAILOR FRIEND once said to me, "You know, the funny thing about the horizon is that you never get to it. You look at it and sail towards it all the time, but it just keeps moving away as you supposedly get closer to it."

That's how it is with many life and career goals. The closer you get to them, the more they seem to diminish in importance. New goals and objectives take the place of the old. That's how it should be. We aren't static beings. George Bernard Shaw put it like this:

> *To have succeeded is to have finished one's business on earth, like the male spider who is killed by the female the moment he has succeeded in his courtship. I like the state of continual becoming, with a goal in front and not behind.*

So many people spend their lives on treadmills, pumping away and getting nowhere. They keep moving, but they never change and grow. They've lost, or maybe just mislaid, that most human of qualities, the ability to change and evolve into something more than they were before.

There are always going to be failures along the way; that's a penalty you pay for taking risks. I like the comment Jesse Jackson made in his speech before the Democratic National Convention in 1988. Speaking of his own failings, he told the assembled group, "Be patient with me. God isn't finished with me yet." But I think that, although God—or whatever you believe in beyond yourself—is going to help, we shouldn't hang around waiting for Him to do all the heavy lifting. We need to take an active hand in developing our own lives and careers.

Can You Keep Loving Your Job?

A job isn't static, and neither are you. Even the most lovable job won't remain lovable if it doesn't grow along with you. And even the most successful employees won't remain successful unless they change too. It's a balancing act—or maybe a juggling act.

You'll have your ups and downs in any job—boring times, stressful times, and wonderfully challenging and satisfying times. There are certain special qualities you can develop in yourself that will make you more likely to succeed at, and love, your job—qualities like sensitivity to other people's dreams and feelings, an ability to plan ahead and keep working towards your goals, and a willingness to take chances and throw yourself with energy and passion into your job.

Probably the most important quality is the ability to accept, and even welcome, change in our jobs, and in ourselves. In many ways, the relationship between you and a job you love is like the relationship between two people in a marriage: two entities that expand and challenge each other, and that sometimes irritate each other. Like the best marriages, the best job matches force each side to grow and change. The fact that *you*—the unique person that you are—do a particular job gives that job a special life and character. It makes your job your own special creation.

Five Ways to Grow in Your Job

These simple little rules and few.

Hilaire Belloc
More Beasts for Worse Children

IN MY WORK with organizations that are struggling with hiring, firing, developing, and sometimes ignoring their employees, I see, again and again, certain characteristic patterns of success and failure on the job. Whatever the business—large or small, manufacturing or service, structured or open, successful or struggling—the people who do best, in terms of promotions, job satisfaction, and personal respect, share certain "success factors." These factors determine, not only whether a person will get ahead at work, but also whether that person will truly love the work they do. Throughout the rest of this section, we'll suggest ways for you to develop and nurture these factors within yourself.

1. *Learn how to cooperate.*

We learned as young children to watch out for other people's feelings, but many of us have forgotten how. Our competitive educational process doesn't teach us very well how to work together and share rewards. The most successful all-round workers are those who remember that they're not in their jobs, or their lives, alone. Other people have dreams, goals, and hopes for their careers and their lives. People who have learned how to work and live with others ask other people what they think and feel. They help others get ahead. They recognize the contributions of other people. They apologize when necessary. And they truly care.

2. *Learn how to communicate.*

When I work with managers who need to fire or lay off people, they tell me, in at least 75 percent of the cases, that these people "lack communication skills." The ability to communicate effectively is the single best predictor of success in management, and in many other types of jobs as well. You don't necessarily need to be a dynamic public speaker—although a few jobs may demand it—but you need to know how to say what you mean (both in person and in writing), to enlist the support of others, and to give and get feedback effectively. Most importantly, you need to listen. My mother used to tell me that's why we have two ears and only one mouth!

3. *Keep learning and growing in your job.*

Successful people aren't complacent. They're interested in broadening their experience and growing into new areas. They're always trying to expand their areas of expertise and responsibility—not because they're "empire builders," but because they have a genuine curiosity and a desire to explore beyond their current territories. They keep exercising their brains. They take classes, go to seminars, read a lot, ask questions, and don't hesitate to try out new possibilities.

4. *Keep plugging.*

Things don't always go the way we wish they would. The people who get the most out of their jobs know how to look beyond today's disappointments and ask:

> What have I learned from this experience?
> How can I do better next time?

They're patient. They know how to stick to their long-term goals without letting short-term setbacks destroy their confidence.

5. *Enjoy both your time at work and your time away from work.*

The most successful people aren't workaholics. They love what they do at work. Not only is their work gratifying professionally, they have fun with it. But they aren't obsessed with their work. They don't exclude everything else. They also know how to love and nurture the other parts of their lives. They recharge their batteries so they can go back to work refreshed. They take time out for their families, their communities, and themselves.

Keep Challenging Yourself

Providence has hidden a charm in difficult undertakings which is appreciated only by those who dare to grapple with them.

Anne-Sophie Swetchine
The Writings of Madame Swetchine

WHEN YOU WERE HIRED into the job of your dreams, you were a certain person, with a certain set of goals and skills. Now, a year later or five years later, you've changed. Your job has changed. You've got to find a way to change and adjust and grow—not despite, but because of, the changes that take place.

When people tell me they hate their jobs, their reasons are almost always some combination of boredom, on the one hand, and stress and anxiety, on the other. In *Flow: The Psychology of Optimal Experience*, Dr. Mihaly Csikszentmihalyi[6] elegantly addresses this duality. He studies the states of "optimal experience," times when people are fully enjoying and involved in what they are doing. What makes an experience genuinely enjoyable—whether at work or in some other arena—is a state of consciousness he calls "flow," a state in which

> . . .*people are so involved in an activity that nothing else seems to matter; the experience is so enjoyable that people will do it at great cost, for the sheer sake of doing it.*

Wouldn't you like to be able to describe your job in this way?

Dr. Csikszentmihalyi reports that most "optimal experiences" involve performing a challenging activity that requires skills. He writes,

> *Flow activities lead to growth and discovery. One cannot enjoy doing the same thing at the same level for long. We grow bored or frustrated; and then the desire to enjoy ourselves again pushes us to stretch our skills, or to discover new opportunities for using them.*

How does flow research translate to the workplace? If your level of skill outstrips the challenge of your work, you're going to be bored. On the other hand, if the challenges of your work outstrip your skills, you're going to be anxious and stressed out. People who truly love their jobs are those whose work continues to provide a good balance between their level of skill and the level of challenge that confronts them.

Consider the case of Fran Wilkins, a newly appointed manager of reimbursement for a large hospital. Fran previously held a similar job at a much smaller hospital, and she's delighted to have moved up to a teaching hospital with more pay and more responsibilities. Will she love her job? You might think so, but it's not a sure thing. Consider Fran in four different situations.

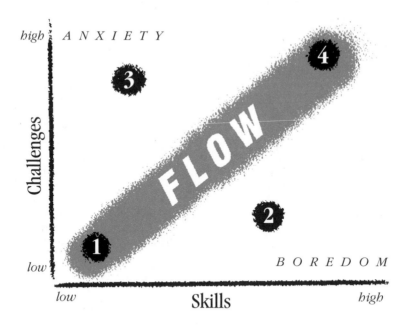

high | ANXIETY

Challenges

low

FLOW

BOREDOM

low   Skills   high

1 For the first few weeks in her new job, Fran is busy getting acclimated. She's challenged, but not overwhelmed, and she's enjoying her new job quite a bit.

2 A few more months go by. Fran's skills are improving, but the challenge of her assignment is staying about the same. Fran is starting to get bored.

3 The state legislature passes health care reimbursement legislation requiring new reports and new documentation. Fran's department is going to have to work hard to change its procedures and paperwork. The situation could eventually result in dramatically reduced revenues to the hospital; the hospital's survival might even be threatened. Fran feels very anxious about her ability to do what needs to be done. How can she get back into balance?

4 Fran buckles down and works hard to meet the challenge. With the help of some health care consultants and the willing support of her staff, she gets the new procedures under control.

Continuing to master and be challenged by your job requires hard work by both you *and* your organization. Fran is willing to work hard, but she can't succeed without the willingness of her organization to be patient with her and to hire expert help when needed.

The happiest and most successful people are those who follow their dreams and use their skills in an industry, a company, and a job role in which these dreams and skills can thrive. Those people with big dreams who find, through luck or design, jobs that nourish and appreciate those dreams will truly love their jobs!

What if your dreams are too big for your job? What if you're changing and growing like crazy, and your job just can't keep up with you? A person with your capacity for growth will have the courage to look for a new job or even a new career.

Use The Team Approach

People change and forget to tell each other.

Lillian Hellman
Toys in the Attic

THE JOB YOU LOVE is going to change; if it doesn't, you're not going to keep loving it. But, although change is necessary, it can also be stressful and threatening. Coping with change in a way that both fulfills you and helps your organization requires that you work creatively together.

Elizabeth Koch was the third employee hired into a two-person publishing company. She stuck with the company as it grew to 120 employees and many millions in sales. Elizabeth gave her all to the company, yet there came a time when Elizabeth felt she'd lost the faith of her boss and her own commitment to the company's future. What had changed?

As the company had grown and diversified, many new employees joined the company, at salaries higher than Elizabeth's. She began to feel that her loyalty and hard work, beyond the call of duty for many years, had not been rewarded. Elizabeth's boss, Ed Myers, noticed the difference in her morale and wanted to work with her to improve the situation.

Elizabeth and Ed finally talked seriously about their feelings about the company. It turned out that money was not the true source of dissatisfaction. The publishing company was now a different place from the small, casual, everybody-do-everything organization Elizabeth and Ed had built from scratch. For better or for worse, they'd grown up. New people were being hired for their professional expertise in new areas—and were being paid accordingly. And yet, Elizabeth still had a wealth of knowledge and experience to contribute to the "new" company, and her valuable history was being wasted. Ed realized that, in his rush to hire new people and build the business, he'd failed to show appreciation to the people who had made the company what it was today—and he had failed to help them grow in the new organization.

How could Elizabeth's invaluable experience and company commitment be put to best use in the future? Together, Ed and Elizabeth came up with a solution that made sense for them and the company. Elizabeth would take over the growing customer support area, where she would share, with both customers and other employees, her experience with all aspects of the company's history and mission. As "the voice of the company," she would use her skills, energy, and willingness to do what it takes to make the customers happy and the company flourish.

54

Can You Face the Reality of Change in Your Job?

You can no more hold back change or progress than you can hold back a river. You may succeed in slowing it or damming it for a while, but eventually the river always wins.

Dr. Alan B. Sostek

SO MANY PEOPLE rebel against changes in their working lives. "Just when I've got it all figured out, they change the rules," they say. And yet, change is not only inevitable, it's instrumental to our growth—in our jobs and in our lives.

My long-time mentor and friend, Dr. Alan Sostek, and I were asked to consult at a suburban hospital several years ago. Fred Cox, the CEO, told us that he and his staff were feeling overwhelmed by the changes taking place in the health care profession. New drugs, billing procedures, insurance carriers, hiring practices, waste disposal techniques, legal liabilities, quality control procedures—it was hard to keep track, let alone to understand the consequences of all these changes and to integrate them into the hospital's current systems. Things were moving faster and faster. Fred was afraid that the pace of change was becoming so great that his staff wouldn't be able to keep up, and that the stress they were already feeling would build until many of his people burned out completely. Should he hire more staff? How should he train the people in his department? Was there a sensible solution?

When we actually talked to the people involved, we found that, although many of them felt overwhelmed at times, most of them enjoyed the challenge and hectic pace of their work. One of them, Mary Beth Poulos, said to us, "All these new things make life here more interesting. I really look forward to coming to work every day!"

Rather than recommending a lot of new hires, Dr. Sostek and I focused on developing a training program that helped people develop, not only the skills to handle changes in hospital procedures, but the willingness to accept the notion of future changes as well.

Change is fundamental to all life, including our life at work. The most human of all traits is the need to modify the world we live in. Coming to terms with change—even welcoming it and responding to it with enthusiasm—is actually a sure way not to burn out.

Can You Change Your Mind?

The greatest discovery of my generation is that a human being can alter his life by altering his attitudes of mind.

William James

HOW CAN YOU FIND a job that you truly love? How can you make the job you have truly lovable? You might need to make a big move: leave your current job, go back to school, search your heart and the job market for just the right match. But sometimes it's not that hard. Learning to love your job may be as easy as adjusting your attitude:

- About what you do every day—Every job has good days and bad, good parts and bad. You don't need to love every task you do every time you do it as long as you know, in your heart, that you're on the right track. You *will* love a job that grows with you, that uses your brain and your heart, and that lets you be your best self. If your job has those fundamental qualities about it, you can ignore petty annoyances, bad days, occasional periods of being overwhelmed, and more.

- About who you work with—You don't need to love everybody in your office or organization. You *do* need to win the respect of those around you, and to give them back the same respect. In the best jobs, the people around you will challenge you to do your best work, will encourage you to express yourself, and will become true colleagues and friends. But you can still love a job without revering everybody you interact with every day. Being an adult means being able to work productively with people you don't always agree with.

You can't hypnotize yourself into loving a hateful job filled with hateful people—nor should you! You have a right to find a job that you truly love. But you've got to be realistic. You won't love every minute of any job. You need to cut through the petty problems and daily annoyances and look at the fundamentals: Is your job basically challenging, satisfying, and even a little bit fun? If it is, then concentrate on enjoying and developing the good parts, improving or eliminating the bad parts, and thinking positive.

Are You Stuck or
Are You Pedaling Slowly?

I'm not stuck in this job. I'm using it as a stepping stone.

Bill Jackson, manager of a shoe shine stand

MANY PEOPLE HAVE JOBS that aren't intrinsically lovable, but they give something special to these jobs nevertheless. Some janitors hate their jobs—and it shows. Others love their jobs, or have come to terms with them, for a variety of good reasons. Here are some of them:

> I'm doing it to make money while I go to school.
>
> It gives me a lot of time to think.
>
> It may not the best job in the world, but they're paying me to work, and I'm going to do a good job.

There are tradeoffs in every job and every life. For you, right now, a job you love may not be an option. You may have to do the best you can with the job you have.

Every job has room for accomplishment and pride. Even in jobs that aren't "power jobs," you can care about quality. You can connect with your fellow workers. You can give something special to the job. Remember that old adage, "Anything worth doing is worth doing well." It's true; both you and your employer will benefit from your efforts.

Every job gives you a chance to build your skills and plan for the future. If your current job doesn't let you use your brain the way you wish it would, take a night class or a seminar that will help you find a better job. Challenge that ill-used brain, and give yourself hope for the future.

Not long ago, I fell into conversation with Bill Jackson, who runs a shoe shine stand. Bill told me that he had always wanted to run his own business. For now, that business was a shoe shine stand. He was making money and getting valuable experience while he worked on his degree at a city college. Lots of us think of shoe shining as a menial job, but Bill didn't have a menial attitude. He listened to the people whose shoes he shined, and he learned bits and pieces about the world of business. Bill told me he knew that many people looked down on him. "They don't know what's going on inside my head, though," he said. "Every day I'm earning more and learning more." By putting money in his pocket, and new ideas in his head, he was, bit by bit, getting closer to his ultimate goal of running a bigger and more professional business.

Keep Learning

If a man neglects education, he walks lame to the end of his life.

Plato
Phaedo

WHAT YOU PUT IN YOUR HEAD nobody can take away from you. People who keep learning tend to be more successful—in their work and in their personal and social lives—than those who do not. Acquiring specific skills, as well as gaining knowledge simply for the sake of knowledge, will help you excel in your career, prepare you to change jobs or even professions, and truly make you a happier, more interested, and more interesting person.

Often, the most accomplished and successful people—people who seem to have it made with the skills they have now—are the ones who keep learning and growing and changing. Bill Cosby was already an admired actor and multimillionaire when he decided to go back to school to get his doctorate. He didn't have a plan for his degree; he just knew that learning was important to him, and he believed that he'd somehow find a way to incorporate what he learned into his work in the future. What he learned in the area of moral education created new themes for Cosby's Fat Albert routines and cartoons, and ultimately the concept behind *The Cosby Show*.

Norm Abram, whose house design and rebuilding skills are profiled in public television's *This Old House* series, decided some years ago that he wanted to become an expert cabinet maker and woodworker. He was already a successful carpenter and media figure, but his love of fine wood and craftsmanship pushed him to achieve a higher level of quality work. He did it for the love of it, but he's also been able to incorporate his new skills into his existing television work, and he created a second show, *The New Yankee Workshop*.

An Exercise in Learning

1. Picture your dream job or a project goal at work. Figure out one specific skill or ability that would help you prepare for that job or project? Typing? Word processing? Accounting? Cooking? Using power tools? Public speaking? The Japanese language? Car repair?

2. Find out where you can acquire this skill. A college course? A training seminar? A book?

3. What have you always wanted to learn how to do—just for fun? Woodworking? Scuba diving? Skydiving? Ballet? Pet grooming? Mystery writing? Parasailing?

4. Find out where you can learn this skill.

5. Now get going. Decide what you're going to learn—whether it's business or pleasure—and go learn it!

Keep Filling Your Toolbox

Tous les jours, à tous points de vue, je vais de mieux en mieux.
Every day, in every way, I am getting better and better.

Emile Coué
Formula in his clinic in France

NO MATTER HOW SATISFYING your current job is, keep filling your toolbox with new skills. There was a time when a job was for life. These days, people don't stay in the same job—or even the same industry—forever. The Bureau of Labor Statistics predicts that a student graduating from college in the year 2000 will change jobs more than ten times during his or her working life and will make five changes in career. You need to be prepared to make these changes because you want to and because they benefit you, not because you're forced into them.

The world is changing, and you've got to change, at least mentally, along with it. The brain is like any other muscle. You need to exercise it, or it will get flabby. If you don't keep learning, and keep changing, you're going to be history, along with cold type, vacuum tube computers, and the U.S.S.R. The story of how computers have revolutionized the world of work in the past thirty years is well-known. But you may not realize how quickly other professions are springing up and changing character—new communications tools, desktop publishing techniques, biotechnology products, CD-ROM, video disk, and other information and entertainment media.

I call learning new tricks and new trades "filling the toolbox" because everything you learn is a tool, something that will serve you at some time in the future—in your own job, in a new job or profession, or even in your retirement years. My father is a plumber, and hey, water, pipes, and wrenches haven't changed a whole lot in quite a while, have they? But, at age 70, my dad's toolbox contains very different tools from the ones he carried around even five or ten years ago. He's always finding new tools to do the job just a little bit better.

You can't stand still even if you want to. To keep employed, even at a minimal level, secretaries who were trained on typewriters have had to learn computers and word processing. Human Resources people have had to keep up with the latest federal rules for equal employment. You've got to keep filling your toolbox, learning to do your current job better, and acquiring skills that will serve you in a better job or a different job in the future.

An Exercise in Filling Your Toolbox

Here are some suggestions for filling your toolbox:

1. Get that next degree, whether it's a Ph.D., an M.S., a B.S., or a G.E.D.

2. Take a continuing education course at your local university, college, junior college, or vocational/technical school. Learn something related to your job or another job you'd like to have.

3. Take any training courses sponsored by your employer.

4. Get into a federal, state, or industry-sponsored apprenticeship program in your field or another one that interests you.

5. Take a home correspondence course.

6. Attend a technical seminar or training session, sponsored by your professional society, a civic association, or an independent training company.

7. Get certified by the certification or accreditation organization for your field. If you're a real estate agent or thinking of being one, contact the National Association of Real Estate Appraisers. If you're interested in massage, contact the National Association of Massage Therapists. Just about every profession has a society that monitors and often certifies the training and performance of its practitioners.

8. Read your professional society's journal and newsletters, as well as occasional textbooks, the daily newspaper, *The Wall Street Journal*, and other news and professional publications you enjoy.

9. Attend a convention, conference, or exhibition sponsored by your professional society.

10. Do some volunteer work that lets you do something—or learn something—you'd like to do on the job.

11. And don't forget to learn something completely unrelated to your job—just because you want to!

Branch Out

L'éducation nous fait ce que nous sommes.
Education makes us what we are.

C.A. Helvétius
Discours

YOU NEVER KNOW where an interest will lead you. Often, learning a new skill related to your profession will make you more successful in that profession. Sometimes, learning something outside your profession—something you love to do—may lead you to a new job that you'll truly love. The most successful people are able to consolidate what they've done in the past with the new skills they acquire. Somebody, somewhere, makes a living doing the "fun" things in life. It could be you!

Consider Lee Henniker, who made her living doing legal and environmental research, but whose first love was running. She volunteered to organize a triathlon in her city. The race got a lot of publicity, and a video recording studio was hired to do some promotional work. Lee worked closely with the video technicians and quickly learned the basics about recording and editing. She was fascinated with the process, got some additional training, and acquired some equipment of her own. At some point, she decided to combine what she knew with what she loved. She now has a small company that videotapes legal depositions, and she's expanding into offering video inventories of home possessions for insurance records.

Mark Weinberg ran a promising business videotaping weddings. At one reception, held at a country club, he found himself tempted to play golf, for the first time in his life, just because the greens looked so beautiful. To his amazement, after he took a few lessons he found that he had a real talent for golf. He worked at the game for several years, met a lot of people, and decided that the golf world was the right place for him. Eventually, he found a job working as an assistant pro, and although he was making a lot less money than he'd earned in the video business, he was happier than he'd ever been in his life.

Pick a skill or an area of study that you love, just because you love it, even if you don't think you need it to make that next career move. You can't always predict what skills you'll need next in your profession, but you can be sure that you'll have a fair chance of being good at the things you love to do. There's another good reason for challenging yourself in a new area. Mastering any new skill—even one not directly relevant to what pays the bills—will increase your overall sense of competence and confidence.

Ask, Ask, Ask

Nothing is given so profusely as advice.

François, Duc de la Rochefoucauld
Reflections, or Sentences and Moral Maxims

IF YOU ARE CONTEMPLATING a major change in your current job, you'll find that other people who do the job you're considering are a great source of information and support.

Jane Parker worked for a large computer firm as a Human Resources training manager. She assessed the needs for training within the company by working with managers throughout one division within the company; she hired trainers and set up training sessions; and she conducted some training sessions herself. Jane was excellent at her job, and she loved the variety it offered. She was so good at her job that one day she was offered the job of Director of Human Resources for the whole division.

Jane was tempted by the increased money and responsibility, but she had never aspired to the job, and she was concerned about the Peter Principle. Was she being promoted to her level of incompetence? She decided to take some time before accepting the new job to find out, as best she could, what it would be like to do that job.

She asked these questions:

What exactly would I be doing in the new job?
Who, within my company, is doing this job or one similar to it?
Who, outside my company, is doing a similar job?

Through her professional organization, the American Society for Training and Development, she even located some people who had made the same transition from training manager to Human Resources director.

The more Jane questioned the specific job offer and thought about her options for the future, the clearer her own goals became. She realized that if she were to leave the job she loved, she would want to leave to become an independent training consultant, not a higher-level manager with extensive management and budgeting responsibility. Ultimately, she decided that the ideal compromise would be to stay in her current job but try to expand her current responsibilities—in particular, training in other technical areas—in a way that would better prepare her for an eventual career as an independent trainer.

Write It Down

Suit the action to the word.

William Shakespeare
Hamlet

MANY OF US make New Year's resolutions. Writing down these resolutions for the next year somehow helps to make our promises tangible.

Athletes sometimes use words—both written and spoken—to motivate and encourage them. Figure skating coach Julie Graham helped one young skater, Kristin Russell, overcome her fear of competition by making the girl write 1000 times, "I am better than I think I am." Together, coach and student tacked the pages containing these phrases to the rink boards each practice session, while Kristin practiced her jumps and routines, and they carried them to competitions throughout the girl's rewarding amateur career.

Words can speed you on your way to success at work, too. Make your own goals more real by putting them on paper. Write a business plan for your success. What are your goals—for this month, this year, the next five years, your life? Rewrite them from time to time. List the ten goals you want to accomplish within the next year. Each time you accomplish one, take out your list, cross off your new accomplishment, and consider adding another goal to the bottom of the list.

An Exercise in Thinking Success

The advertisers know the power of repetition. We hear their messages all day. "You deserve a break today." "Reach out and touch someone." "Be all you can be."

Children who are told frequently, "You're smart, you're going to be able to solve this problem," do much better in school than those who aren't given these positive messages. Unfortunately, the world probably isn't going to encourage us and give us the pep talks we need. We're going to have to do it ourselves. Nobody is going to write *your* slogan but you.

A Note To Skeptics: This exercise may seem awfully silly. But I find that people who want to become successful have a better chance of making it when they do exercises of this kind. They have slogans, they have posters on their walls, they have tapes they listen to, they have heroes they try to emulate. Overcome your cynicism. Just try it!

1. Take the following phrase:

    "As far as work goes, I want to…"

2. Now, complete the sentence. Don't think about it too much. Just say what you really want. Not what you think you should want. Not what your boss or family wants you to want. Just you. If you can't write it in a sentence, you can't get anyone to give it to you, that's for sure.

3. Finally, add these words onto your sentence:

    "…and I can!"

4. Read this sentence out loud five times right now. Read it again five times before you go to bed, five times when you wake up in the morning, and five times at lunch. Keep reading it until it's a part of you.

Be a Realistic Optimist

The optimist proclaims that we live in the best of all possible worlds; and the pessimist fears this is true.

James Branch Cabell
The Silver Stallion

THE PHRASE "realistic optimist" may sound like an oxymoron—like "jumbo shrimp" or "deafening silence," but it's not. We all know what an optimist is: someone who is always looking on the bright side, one who believes that things will work out for the best. A pessimist, on the other hand, is one who's much more likely to look on the dark side, one who believes that things will *not* work out well.

In 1914, when Thomas Edison was 67 years old, Edison Laboratories in New Jersey burnt almost to the ground, and he lost $2 million (in 1914 dollars) in equipment, as well as the records and files from the work of much of his lifetime. The next morning, walking with his son through the charred ruins, Edison said, "There is great value in disaster. All our mistakes are burned up. Thank God we can start anew!" This may sound like mindless optimism, but Edison knew he had the perspective and the technical know-how to be able to start again.

Optimists definitely fare better in life. In *Learned Optimism,*[7] Dr. Martin E.P. Seligman explores how optimists do better in school, work, sports, and love. They experience better health, recover more quickly when they do get sick, and even live longer.

We live in an imperfect world—one in which innocent people are cheated, love is betrayed, airplanes crash, and the best applicant doesn't always get the job. Should these situations make you a pessimist? Absolutely not! But they should point out why I use the adjective "realistic" to temper the word "optimist." Dr. Seligman puts it this way: "Life inflicts the same setbacks and tragedies on the optimist as on the pessimist, but the optimist weathers them better."

Realistic optimism is an ability to combine positive thinking with a dose of realism. Realistic optimists don't see only the bright side. They look at both sides of a situation and then figure out a way to make the best of either one. Seeing both sides of a situation isn't easy. When we're faced with disappointment and disillusionment, it's natural to be consumed with painful feelings. Realistic optimists don't ignore the feelings, but, like Edison, they use all their resources to pick up the pieces and move on.

An Exercise in Realistic Optimism

1. List a few of your most significant accomplishments. Did they come easily or with difficulty? How did you feel when you accomplished them? How did you spur yourself on? Can you use the same motivational techniques to reach your new objectives at work?

2. List a few of the worst things that have happened to you—at work or in the other parts of your life. For each of them, think of at least one thing you learned from the experience that will help you in the future.

3. Each time you look at a new situation, ask yourself:

    What is the worst possible outcome of this situation?

    What are the odds that this situation will turn out that badly?

    What action steps can I take to reduce those odds?

4. Next, ask yourself:

    What is the best possible outcome of this situation?

    What are the odds that this situation will turn out that well?

    What action steps can I take to increase those odds?

5. Finally, ask yourself:

    Do I have to do this alone, or is there someone who has traveled this road before?

    Would that person be willing to help me?

    Can that person show me some of the potholes to avoid?

Learn To Think Positive

'Twixt the optimist and pessimist
The difference is droll:
The optimist sees the doughnut
But the pessimist sees the hole.

McLandburgh Wilson
Optimist and Pessimist

HOW CAN YOU BECOME a realistic optimist? Is it inborn or can you develop this habit of mind? With the state of the economy, the environment, and society in general, isn't pessimism (and its evil stepchild, depression) the only sensible response to the events around us? No, it doesn't need to be. If you are willing to spend some of your time and energy, there are proven psychological methods for improving your outlook on life.

In *Learned Optimism,* Dr. Seligman describes very well how many of us learn passivity and helplessness, and he makes a strong case for learning to think more positively. I believe firmly that if you can learn to think more positively about yourself and the world around you, you'll handle the things that happen in your life with greater verve and success.

On the pages that follow is an exercise adapted, with the permission of the author, from Dr. Seligman's exercises in Learned Optimism. *In that book Dr. Seligman develops the A-E elements, based partly on the pioneering work of Dr. Albert Ellis, author of* A Guide to Rational Living, *and other works. I've modified those elements a bit, and contributed the F and G elements.*

You need to remember seven words, beginning with the first seven letters of the alphabet. On the first page of the exercise, I've defined the seven words; on the next two, I've included an exercise sheet on which one of my clients has completed each item. Take a look at these and then try your own exercise.

This exercise may sound like psychological mumbo-jumbo, but most people who can suspend their disbelief are surprised by how successful the exercise can be. Even if you think you're just playing tricks on yourself, give it a try. What do you have to lose, except your depression? (For many more examples of how you can use such exercises at work, school, and home, see Dr. Seligman's book.)

ABCDEFG WORKSHEET: Some Definitions

A **Adversity** is something bad that happens to you. It happens to optimists, pessimists, the good guys, the bad guys, and everybody in between. When you're faced with a negative situation, don't blow it out of all proportion. Gather your composure and write down a brief, unemotional description of the facts.

B **Beliefs** are developed, almost automatically, from both positive and negative events. They represent what you *think* about these events, and how you interpret them.

C **Consequences** are the feelings the event causes and the action(s) you take because of them.

D **Disputation** is the technique of positive self-talk. Pretend you have a good, optimistic friend in your corner, giving you solid support. Dispute your negative, pessimistic thinking. Use all your persuasive powers—just as if you were arguing with somebody else. Really get into it. An easy way to remember how to make your persuasion as strong as possible is to remember the vowels, *A, E, I, O, U*:

    A   What are the other **Alternatives**, or contributing causes to the adversity?

    E   What actual **Evidence** strengthens your case?

    I   What are the **Implications** of your negative belief, whether or not it's true?

    O   While you're using all your powers of intellect and concentration, don't forget to look at the **Obvious Outcomes**?

    U   How productive or **Useful** is it for you to continue to dwell on your adversity and your feelings about it?

E **Energization** is the flow of positive energy you receive from dealing with—and getting rid of—negative beliefs. Key in to the difference between how you were feeling before you began this exercise (when the event you're describing first occurred) and how you're feeling now (as you work to address the event and your feelings about it).

F **Future Action** is your plan for concrete, positive behavior that will reinforce a more positive outlook in the future. It's not enough just to work on your feelings and deal with your pessimistic reactions in an intellectual way. You need to act!

G **Gain** is the positive reinforcement you'll receive when you react to adversity and change your pessimistic outlook. What's in it for you to change your approach? The gain can be internal or external, monetary or not, from yourself or from others, etc.

ABCDEFG WORKSHEET: A Real Example

A **Adversity:** This is the third time in recent memory that my immediate supervisor took credit for something I thought of. He never gives me any credit!

B **Beliefs:** My boss doesn't care if I get recognized for my work. My boss is unfair to me. I'll never get ahead in this company.

C **Consequences:** I am angry and frustrated that my boss is such a sleazy jerk. I didn't say anything to him because I don't want to shoot myself in the foot, but this is the last time I'm bringing a good idea to him.

D **Disputation:**

  A **Alternatives:** Maybe my boss wasn't sure this was such a good idea, and didn't want me to get blamed. Maybe he did mention my contribution and I just don't know about it. Maybe this idea has been tried before and there's some history I don't know about.

  E **Evidence:** My boss does like my work. I know this because he gave me a raise at my last review and a good Christmas bonus. Some additional evidence: I've received two promotions over the past four years.

  I **Implications:** Even if my boss doesn't want me to get ahead or care about my getting ahead, I may still be able to get ahead without him. I've got be careful how I do it. If he's treated other people this way, maybe it's obvious to upper management that he hogs the limelight. It's probably also obvious to others at my level. I should inquire about this in a discreet way.

  O **Obvious Outcomes:** If I don't ever suggest new ideas, I'll hurt myself too.

  U **Useful:** If I keep thinking about what a creep this guy is, who knows what I might say to him. That would really mess things up.

E   Energization: I'm more in control of myself and the situation now that I've had a chance to think about it. Maybe my boss doesn't care about me, but maybe there are other reasons for what's been happening. I'm feeling a little better realizing that there's no law that I have to continue to work for him.

F   Future Action: I will find a good time to talk to my boss and find out whether or not he's been giving me credit. Also, I will discreetly ask around to see if any of my coworkers have had these experiences. If I end up really believing that I'm being blocked, I'm going to make some moves. One idea is to get myself on a multi-department task force where I'll be observed (and maybe recruited) by somebody else in the company. Another idea is to join a professional association so I can start expanding my network outside the company in case I decide to leave.

G   Gain: If I deal with this situation in a more positive way, I'll be less anxious about my relationship with my boss. I may or may not like him any better, but at least I'll know where I stand. I may be able to leverage this new understanding on my part into a better role within this company. At the very least, it's forcing me to do something about this situation so I'll feel better about myself.

Say No to Nay-Sayers

It is easy—terribly easy—to shake a man's faith in himself.

George Bernard Shaw
Candida

THE PEOPLE AROUND US affect our emotions and our motivation. That's one reason parents of teenagers are often concerned about who their children spend time with. For generations, teenagers have been saying, "But everybody else is doing it," and parents have been saying, "If everybody else jumped off a cliff, would you?" The answer, very likely, is yes!

The peer group is a powerful influence—on adults as well as teenagers. Who you spend time with makes a big difference to your mental attitude and your emotions. Happy, helpful people give you a boost. Gloomy or angry people are bound to drag you down with them.

If you have a choice, try to stay away from people who are pessimistic and unenergetic. I'm not talking about good friends who are going through a bad time. Of course you need to be there for them for as long as they need you. I'm talking about the professional whiners. These are the coworkers who always complain, who always blame someone—their managers or subordinates, the marketing department or the salespeople or the accounting department, their mother or their kids. These people are the kiss of death for productivity and happiness in an organization. Keep your distance. There are lots of happy, positive, energetic people out there. Hang out with them.

Heroes Aren't Just for Comic Books

Lives of great men all remind us
We can make our lives sublime,
And, departing, leave behind us
Footprints on the sands of time.

Henry Wadsworth Longfellow
Resignation

TO BE SUCCESSFUL —in life and in business—you need to feel successful. And you need to have some heroes. Who are your heroes? Who genuinely inspires you? Don't be afraid to be uncool. If John F. Kennedy, Lee Iacocca, Bonnie Blair, or someone in your own family inspires you, let them work for you. Put their pictures up on the walls of your office (or inside a drawer if you're embarrassed). Read their books, listen to tapes of their speeches, and watch their movies. All the positive messages of their lives and works will inspire you to achieve your own glory.

Athletes know how to use their own heroes to their best advantage. Competitors use all kinds of motivational tricks to pump themselves up and prepare to do their best. Sometimes these tricks are hokey and the athletes know it, but they also know this stuff sometimes works. David Santee, a contender for a gold medal in figure skating around the time of the 1980 Olympics, found himself faltering when it mattered the most. He devised a motivational system based on watching the *Rocky* movie and listening to the music from the movie while he waited to compete. He knew he was playing tricks on himself, but he also knew that Rocky and his prizefights could help him fight his own demons.

Practice Heroism Every Day

Modern industry needs visionary heroes more than ever before,
not only to build new worlds, but also to invent better mousetraps.

Terrence E. Deal and Allen A. Kennedy
Corporate Cultures

YOU CAN BE A HERO, TOO! As kids, we all had heroes—and we all wanted to be heroes too. When did we decide that it was immature or uncool or, that worst of business sins, unrealistic, to want to be a hero—to make an indelible mark, reach an unreachable goal, or give to society in a way that would be remembered and would have an impact?

What is a hero? Heroes come in all flavors. They discover a new drug, they rush a friend to the hospital, they share a symphony with the world, they sit and chat with a lonely old veteran in a hospital. They invent new rockets to speed us into outer space, as well as flip-top toothpaste caps that won't fall off and rattle around on the bathroom floor. In short, they make a difference—to their world and to themselves.

In *Corporate Cultures*, Terrence E. Deal and Allen A. Kennedy make a strong case for the need for heroes today—not just in battlefields and rockets and social movements—but in our boardrooms and on our manufacturing floors. Is it incongruous to think of being a hero in your store or department or bus route? A hero makes a mark and sets a standard. You can do this in a burning building. But you can also do it, day by day, in a job. *You* are in charge of making that job what it can be. If you do your job, whatever it is, with a complete investment of energy, brainpower, and spirit, you'll make your heroic mark every day.

When I think of unsung corporate heroes, I remember Ruth Windham, who was put in charge of outplacement at a high-tech company that had been sold to a more successful competitor. When I went to meet with Ruth, I was shocked to find her alone, in a distant corner of what had once been a bustling manufacturing floor. Approaching her office through the immense, empty, echoing expanse was downright spooky. And, of course, outplacement isn't the cheeriest profession even in the most beautiful surroundings. I asked Ruth how she could work under such conditions. "I made good money—in salary and stock—at this company when times were good. They did well by me and I owe them," Ruth told me. "If I hang in here and work with the outplacement company, more of these people will land on their feet." It's easy to work hard at a company that's booming and cheerful. It's a lot harder to hang in there with a company that's on its last legs.

Keep Your Eye on
the Big Picture

The art of being wise is the art of knowing what to overlook.

William James
The Principles of Psychology

SOMETIMES, people who love their jobs can't let go of any piece of them. If you're good at something, if you've taken responsibility for something in the past, it's hard to give it over to somebody else. But sometimes you need to step back from the detail work and broaden your focus.

I worked once with a growing organization in which the marketing manager and the tradeshow coordinator had different views of the coordinator's job role. Kirk Adkins, the tradeshow coordinator, did a wonderful job, putting together tradeshow exhibits for a high-tech company, arranging for staff and materials, and pulling together all of the details necessary to make a show a success. So what was the problem?

The company's marketing manager knew that Kirk could hire staff to do the detail work he'd put in place. She wanted him to think more strategically about how to make the company's tradeshows really successful. She also wanted Kirk to take on some of her responsibilities—to think about ways of improving the shows by analyzing competitors' booths and demos and by dreaming up new gimmicks. She wanted him to find ways of using the company's tradeshow presence to court their biggest customers—maybe by running special VIP events in conjunction with the shows. She wanted him to do an analysis of ways they could split or share staff to allow them to attend even more trade shows.

Kirk didn't see that, in his growing company, continuing to do the same job well wasn't enough. To keep on being successful, he needed to expand his job—to delegate or let go of some of the details, to look at the big picture.

Kirk found it hard to delegate. He had such a vested interest in all the procedures and details he'd mastered that he found it hard to believe that anybody could do the job as well as he could. And, of course, they couldn't—at least not at first. But unless he tried to hand over some of his current responsibilities, he wouldn't be able to take on new ones. And, despite his many past successes, he'd fail to satisfy his boss and continue to be successful in a changing company.

Play the Long Game

Ah! que la vie est quotidienne.
Oh! What a day-to-day business life is.

Jules LaForgue
Complainte sur certains ennuis

THE PHRASE "play the long game" comes from the game of golf. It's a good phrase, I think, because it suggests the difference between someone who's great in the clutch, who sprints, who sinks the putt (all valuable qualities), and someone who is enduring, who hangs tough over the long haul, who doesn't have to win the quick victory to keep motivated.

Thomas Edison tried more than 5000 different experiments aimed at finding the right filament for a light bulb, and he kept coming up with elements that burnt out too quickly. His assistants were greatly discouraged, but Edison remained calm and steadfast. At one point, after many unsuccessful attempts, an assistant said in despair, "We've failed again." Edison told him in all seriousness, "We haven't failed at all. We've succeeded in finding another thing that doesn't work. When we've eliminated all these things that don't work, we'll find the one that *does* work."

Paul Tartikoff started out in the maintenance department of a large insurance company. His hard work and energy got him promoted to the mail room, but he was told that without a college degree he couldn't advance further within the company. He was determined to get that degree and, after seven years of night school, he succeeded. The company kept its side of the bargain and made him a management trainee. The same perseverance that he'd demonstrated getting his degree was evident in everything he did, and he advanced quickly through the ranks. Today he manages several hundred people and he loves what he does.

Actor Danny Glover had a serious learning disability as a child. Teachers told his family he was probably retarded and would never hold a job. His mother believed in his intelligence, worked with him daily to find successful learning strategies, and taught him to hang in there despite adversity. Today, the star of the *Lethal Weapon* movies—and many more—reaps the rewards of his mother's belief and his own perseverance.

Perseverance is a virtue and also a necessity. You've got to keep going, one day at a time. The only question is how. Will you trudge along, day by day, depressed and tired of trying? Or will you keep at it, cheerfully sticking to your goal, maybe modifying it bit by bit, and yourself bit by bit, until you reach that goal?

An Exercise in Playing the Long Game

1. Think of something in your life that you quit on—and wish you hadn't.

   How about taking those last two college courses you needed to graduate or to get certified as a teacher? What about writing that resumé for a different type of job?

2. What did you learn from that?

3. What in your life have you really stuck to? How about that car repair course that was so hard at first? How about when your loyalty to your company helped you outlast a really unfair boss? Or those less than honeymoon years in your marriage when the babies had colic and the roof leaked?

4. What did you learn from that?

5. What is frustrating you right now? What are you tempted to quit on?

6. What ideas, resources, and people are there to help you keep at it?

   How about an understanding boss, coworkers, family, and friends? How about a book, a college or adult education course, a motivational seminar, a professional association meeting, or a support group? You might need help in playing the long game. Remember, you're entitled to ask for it.

Play the Waiting Game

I should have found in some part of my soul
A drop of patience.

William Shakespeare
Othello

FRETTING ABOUT how fast you're going isn't going to get you there faster. It's just going to ruin your enjoyment of the journey by making you unhappy, stressed out, and bad-tempered.

We all have to stand in lines. Don't just stand there. Use your time to talk to the guy in front of you or behind you. You can call it networking if you want, or you can just enjoy what he has to say. Observe people and learn something about human nature—and your own. Relax and meditate so you can refresh yourself for when you're out of line. Fantasize. Read a book. Or write one—at least a journal.

We stand in lines in our careers too. Sometimes we may seem to be stuck in a dead-end job. Or we may not be able to make the career moves we want to make. There are certain times in our careers that, try as we will, we won't be able to make much progress. Maybe there just isn't enough room on the job ladder above us. Maybe the economy doesn't allow for raises or expansion. But maybe you're basically happy with your job, and you don't want to make a move. Or it's a bad time personally to change jobs. I'm not telling you to stop trying, just to stop fretting about it. At certain times of life, there's only so much you can do. Try to relax. Now may be the time to get new skills, try a new hobby, and refresh your relationships with other people.

When Susan and Tony Acello were expecting their first child, they thought long and hard about how they'd balance their work and child care responsibilities. They decided that with some juggling they'd both be able to continue working. Then they found out that their baby was twins, and suddenly things weren't so controllable. They couldn't afford day care for two, they didn't feel comfortable with a live-in sitter, and they worried that their babies might need extra attention if they were premature.

After a lot of debate, the Acellos decided that Susan, who managed a large quality assurance department at a manufacturing plant, would return to work full-time after her maternity leave, and Tony, who worked as a technical writer for a small and more flexible company, would try to work out an arrangement that would let him work part-time at home—ideally during off hours when Susan would be home. It wasn't a great solution, but life doesn't always go along with our plans. The Acellos knew the babies wouldn't be babies forever. Now was a time for patience.

An Exercise in Playing the Waiting Game

1. If you feel time is wasting, ask yourself:

    How can I make this time productive?

2. If you find yourself waiting in line a lot, carry:

    A book or magazine you need to read.

    A language or book tape you need to listen to.

    A list you need to rewrite.

    A prayer, a reflection, or even a joke you need to say.

3. Meditate or practice deep breathing techniques to help yourself relax.

4. Look at the sources of your frustration. Identify the time wasters in your life and try to eliminate them, as best you can, so you won't find yourself in so many frustrating situations.

Organizations Need Patience, Too

Our patience will achieve more than our force.

Edmund Burke
Reflections on the Revolution in France

SOMETIMES, an organization needs patience too. Recessionary times can put a business on hold.

At Faxon Motors, a bad economy has cut deeply into the car business, a number of people have been laid off, and the remaining staff are depressed and worried. I did some organizational counseling at the dealership after the layoffs and asked these questions of management and staff:

Management:

> Now that you've made cuts, are you financially able to weather the recession if it lasts a few more years?
> Do you have confidence in the people that remain?

Staff:

> Are you working as hard as you can to make this business successful?
> Do you think the recession will turn around?
> Do you want to be in this business when things do turn around?
> Do you want to be in your current job when things turn around?

This was an easy one. Everybody in management and on the staff answered "yes" to every single question. I had no magic bullet. My basic advice was to hang in there and be patient. Finances were stable, for now. Everybody was doing as much as they could to cut expenses and increase income. The rest was out of their hands, at least for now.

Some things *are* out of our hands, and sometimes it's hard for busy, productive, striving people to face that fact. I was once making a trip with Dr. Alan Sostek. Snow was predicted and we had a long drive ahead of us. I was worrying about the weather—whether we'd have a storm, and whether we'd get there in time, and what would happen if we didn't, and why it was winter, and on and on. Dr. Sostek, who defined stress as "worrying about or trying to control those things we cannot control," finally said to me, "Paul, let God do weather. We do snow tires."

Work Can Be Fun

To love what you do and feel that it matters—how could
anything be more fun?

Katharine Graham
Washington Post

WORK IS GOOD for your soul, your sense of self, and ultimately the world you live in. Because it brings financial, as well as psychological rewards, work is also good for your family, your profession, and even your country. How uplifting! With all this uplift, we sometimes forget that work can simply be fun.

Many people love their jobs—not necessarily because they feel that they're saving humanity or building a new mousetrap. They just have fun doing what they do. I'm not talking about working in a circus or a rodeo. Many people just get enormous enjoyment out of the ordinary tasks they perform each day.

Jane Renquist sells printing services and, for her, every day is fun. "I love what I do," she told me. "I get to see my customers every day—and I like them a lot. I get to meet new people and try to persuade them to be my customers in the future. I get to work with the guys in the shop, and I get to drive around in my car. What could be better?" In recent years, it's become harder than ever to sell printing, and Jane's had to switch jobs a few times in the years I've known her. But she's never considered changing fields. She's broken down what she does each day into its component parts, and she's decided that she likes every one of them. Talking to customers and coworkers suits her outgoing personality. Scrambling for business is a challenge, but one she feels confident she can handle. She even loves to drive! What a great match!

Jane says that some of her friends think she ought to be moving on and up in her field or another one. "Why should I," she asks, "when I'm having such a good time and making enough money for me? Is there some law that I have to do something I hate?"

Laughter and satisfaction lengthen our lives. It's a scientific fact. And hostility and aggression shorten them. If your job is fun for you, count your blessings and keep laughing. Don't be bullied by your parents, your spouse, your coworkers, or even this book into thinking you need to analyze, excel, and strive until you're miserable.

Plan for Tomorrow, but Don't Sacrifice Today

When I went to the Bar as a very young man,
(Said I to myself—said I),
I'll work on a new and original plan,
(Said I to myself—said I).

W.S. Gilbert
Iolanthe

PLANNING IS VITAL to finding and nurturing a job you love. But you can't let the plan get the better of you. A perfectly reasonable plan might be to go to medical school and become a surgeon—but at 50, with five kids, in debt? You may need to temper that plan a bit. They say that the first victim of war is truth. I say it's the plan. Sometimes you've got to compromise and put some limitations on your goals. That doesn't mean you give them up. But it might mean you settle for the right job in the wrong industry, for example—at least for now.

Christa Burns worked as a clerk in the financial services division of an insurance company. She was a tremendously energetic and determined person who wanted to be a high-level executive recruiter. Christa read everything she could, networked with everyone she knew, and still couldn't get a foot in the door. After numerous rejections she decided not to give up but to temper her plan. She lowered her sights a bit and went to work as an internal recruiter in the Human Resources department of a high tech company. She grew in the job and eventually managed the entire department. She confesses to a small amount of satisfaction when the recruiters who turned her down come to her with their candidates.

You also need to be able to take advantage of whatever your current situation is. If your next accounting assignment will take you to Hollywood, grinding out spreadsheets for Steven Spielberg, you may just decide to go for it, even if you've been trying to get out of the spreadsheet business. You'll have to look deep inside yourself to decide whether to adjust your careful plan to make room for a once-in-a-lifetime opportunity—or to turn down the opportunity, however dazzling, and move on to the next phase of your life.

Remember, there are limits to planning. Don't sacrifice the time you have now, always looking to tomorrow. Somebody said, "Life is what happens while you're making plans for the future." Don't be so focused on the future that you don't seize today's opportunities.

An Exercise in Planning Ahead

Write down, even in outline form, your plan—for a new career, a new job, a new project at work, whatever. Make sure you can answer "yes" to all of the following questions.

1. Does it have one over-arching, central goal?

2. Does it have distinct steps or plateaus?

3. Does it have specific activities?

4. Does it have specific "deliverables?"

   Create a certain number of new pieces in your advertising portfolio. Make a certain number of new contacts in your profession. Take a certain number of new course in your area—auto mechanics, computers, accounting, engineering, nursing, management, or whatever.

5. Do you have target dates for accomplishments?

6. Do you regularly update your plan with new data you're gathering?

Build Something That Will Last

The greatest use of life is to spend it for something that will outlast it.

William James

A COMPLAINT I HEAR OFTEN from working people today—even those with high-level professional jobs—is "I'm not doing anything important." They put in their time, they may not mind what they do with that time, and they carry home a paycheck. But they're not doing anything of value, anything that lasts. On the other hand, I know people who are doing low-level, even menial jobs, but feel important because they are working for something of value.

"Something of value" might mean a medical or social program—a hospital job, a volunteer stint at Oxfam, work on a political campaign. Or it might be work in a company that's building a product or providing a necessary service. Morale was very high among the government and corporate people who worked on the Apollo Project that first sent people to the moon. Many people love working for newspapers, magazines, and publishing houses because there is tangible output—words and ideas that may make a difference in people's lives. There is contagious excitement in a company that is building a better mousetrap.

I saw a profound example of this sense of building something of value when I visited the former Soviet Union during the time that the country was unravelling. I got to know Igor Zlotnikov, one of the few management psychologists there. In the midst of poltical chaos and economic privation, he and his colleagues—all psychologists— were laboring to improve conditions at the hospitals, schools and manufacturing plants where they worked. But, in addition to the specific work they did, they understood quite well that by teaching what were to the Soviets new concepts of empowerment, decision-making, and responsibility (ideas contrary to the old notions of centralized control), they were, fundamentally, building a new society.

Some people are discouraged when the goal is a long-term one, or one—like conquering hunger or AIDS—that seems so formidable. But those who can keep focused on a meaningful, long-term goal are often the people who love their jobs the most.

To a large extent, cable TV is the brainchild of Ted Turner, who dreamed of a new television network and found a way to make that dream come true. What made Turner successful? His own father was a small businessman who owned a billboard company and tore the family apart by committing suicide. Yet Turner attributes his success to his father. Says Turner, "He told me to dream a dream that probably couldn't even be accomplished in my lifetime."

You Are Not Your Job

Never allow your sense of self to become associated with
your sense of job. If your job vanishes, your self doesn't.

Gordon Van Sauter
Working Woman, February, 1988

IT'S ONE THING to love your job and revel in doing it every day. It's another to lose yourself completely in that job, or to let that job completely define you. Identify *with* your job, but don't identify yourself *as* that job.

I once knew a judge I'll call Ezra Johnson. Judge Johnson spent all his waking hours judging. Even his posture and his way of greeting people, as if from a great height, were stereotypically judge-like. Used to demanding reasonable doubt and handing down verdicts in the courtroom, he found it difficult to play a different role outside that courtroom. Even in family discussions, he was unemotional, demanding, and rational to the point of harshness—in a word, judgmental. Ezra identified himself so strongly with his job that he carried its trappings—even its stereotypes—into every corner of his life. His wife, children, neighbors, friends, and community acquaintances came to feel that they were on trial in his courtroom, not partners in his life. Ezra was so completely "The Judge" that I can't imagine his life without his robes. This is a case of *being* your job.

Loving your job is a different thing entirely. Loving your job means sharing with that job the special qualities that make you the person you are—and in that way making your job more special too. A priest can be a crook or a saint. A banker can build a community or let it fall apart. It isn't the job that makes the person; it's the person who makes the job. Focus on *who you are* and *what you do*, rather than *what your job is* and *where you do it*.

The danger of over-identifying with a job comes to a head when that job is lost. In times of layoffs and shrinking workforces, many people who love their jobs and have given their all to those jobs are severed from them. If this happens to you, it will be hard not to take it personally. And yet, for so many people a job loss has nothing to do with who you are. Often, it's the result of a cutback or a company reorganization. What happens in a layoff usually happens to your job, not to you. Imagine that a car swerves and hits your car while you're sitting innocently in traffic. That car would have hit anybody sitting in any car in that place at that time. The accident has little to do with you personally. So, take it in stride. Get out and hitch a ride until you can get the car fixed or find a new one.

Focus on Today

Tomorrow is another day.

Scarlett O'Hara, in Margaret Mitchell's
Gone With The Wind

DON'T LET YESTERDAY or tomorrow gnaw on you. Worry as we will about it, we can't live yesterday over, and we can't do anything about tomorrow except live today right. We'll all know tomorrow night how tomorrow turns out.

Back in the 1960s, the traditional wisdom about ulcers was that those who suffered from this ailment needed to avoid spicy or acidic foods. The tomato lobby felt that its favorite food was getting a bum rap, and somehow persuaded the Department of Agriculture to do a study about ulcers, tomatoes, and their link, or lack thereof. In its final report, the DOA included a line I like a lot:

> *Ulcers and other gastrointestinal upsets result not from what we eat but from what's eating us.*

Remember what your grandmother used to say: "Don't frown. Do you want your face to freeze that way?" It's true that people who worry and are anxious tend to look older than those who stay calm and cheerful. As we run from work to the health club in our endless quest to stop the ravages of time, we might take a moment to contemplate the fact that the best thing we can do to keep looking younger is perhaps to stop trying to live three days—yesterday, today, and tomorrow—in every one.

Work You Love Is Never Done

To travel hopefully is a better thing than to arrive,
and the true success is to labour.

Robert Louis Stevenson
El Dorado

SOME OF THE GREATEST success stories of our time never arrived. They kept traveling, enjoying their work and building ever-greater monuments to their own dreams and hard work. Thomas Edison put it this way: "Show me a satisfied man and I will show you a failure."

Sam Walton, who founded the Wal-Mart stores and became, at one time, the richest person in America, is a good example of a dramatically successful man who was never content to rest on his laurels. As successful as he became, he never stopped working and building and enjoying what he had created and what he continued to create.

Sam Walton is also a good example of a great man who never forgot how to talk—and listen—one-on-one with the people who staffed and shopped in his stores. He continued to drive a pickup truck from his home in Arkansas, combining his original down-home charm with a lot of hard-won business acumen. He spent time every week in his stores (now numbering nearly 2000) checking the layout, asking employees how procedures could be improved, and asking customers what they liked and didn't like about the stores and their merchandise. Whenever a new store opened, he'd spend the day there, talking on the loudspeaker, thanking people for working and shopping there. He translated his own good humor into a policy of congeniality in the stores. According to one employer, "A smile is more contagious than a frown, and smiling is a big part of our policy."

What If You Don't Have a Job You Love?

There are many ways to turn the job you have into a job you'll love. But sometimes, you simply can't make it work. Then, it's time to move on.

If you're in a job that doesn't satisfy you, if you've lost your job and desperately need a new one, or if you're in the job market for the first time, you'll have some very important questions to answer:

- What kind of person are you?

- What do you love to do?

- What have you dreamed of doing?

- What are your passions and your happiest memories?

- What field, occupation, and activities bring out the best in you?

Job hunting can be one of the most frightening and demoralizing experiences we undergo. But, try to remember, as you're going through this process, that you're not a beggar, looking for a hand-out of a job—any job. If you can clearly focus in on your dreams, skills, and passions, you'll have the confidence of knowing how much you have to give to the job you're sure to find.

OPP'Y OF A LIFETIME

Fast-growing midtown corp needs bright, articulate M/F to reorganize 760,000 files from top to bottom, fire four people nobody else will, and take care of children aged three and one. Must be certified in UNEX, GOM, SYSCO, CREM, LEM, ZOT, FENIX, JOD, and FRON. Own car a necessity, also up-to-date trucking license. Knowledge of quantum physics, short-order cookery helpful. Can you type? Even better. If you have $250,000 cash and are not afraid of large dogs, we're looking for YOU. At least twelve years' experience required. Personable, attractive college grads only call 555-2121 for appt. Starting salary 9K. Great benefits.

R. Chast

What Do You Know?
What Can You Do?

*Our works are the mirror wherein the spirit first sees its
natural lineaments. Hence, too, the folly of that impossible
precept, 'Know thyself;' till it be translated into this partially
possible one, "Know what thou canst work at."*

Thomas Carlyle
Sartor Resartus

WHAT'S THE FIRST STEP in looking for a job you'll love—whether it's
your first job or your tenth? Start with the want ads, right? Wrong!

Before you can embark on a career that you truly love—a job that satisfies you in ways
far beyond money—you need to look carefully at what you know and what you can
do. You also need to look deeply inside yourself—at what excites you, at what moves
you, at what you love.

Before beginning to build, any craftsperson asks the questions:

What tools do I need for this job?
What tools do I have already?
What tools do I need to acquire before I can get the job done?

You have a toolbox of hard-won skills and personal qualities. Before you can figure
out what work is right for you, you've got to do an inventory. You may not use all your
tools. But you don't know yet what you're going to need. Your first job is to figure out
what's in there.

Most of us undervalue what we know and what we have to offer. You are more than
your job title. Your skills far outstrip those you're currently getting paid to exercise. A
job you love may capitalize more on your education, your avocations, or your passions
than on your specific work skills. So don't limit your inventory of tools to those you use
at the office. Remember, you've been a student, a parent, a spouse, a friend, an athlete,
a member of a community, a part of any number of organizations, and a reader and
learner about all kinds of intellectual and philosophical issues. All those aspects of
your life and personality contribute to making you who you are.

What have you done? What have been your greatest accomplishments? Your greatest
frustrations? What did you like? What do you never want to do again? You've learned a
lot. And you've paid a heavy tuition for your lifetime course in self-knowledge. Make it
pay off now.

Do Your Homework

Take time enough; all other graces
Will soon fill up their proper places.

John Byrom
Advice to Preach Slow

PEOPLE HATE TO HEAR me tell them to take their time and do their homework. They want to get on with it. Enough psychoanalysis! Enough reseach! Where's the resume?

But this self analysis stage is the best investment you can make in a job you'll love. It's better to invest time up front than to spend the rest of your working life in a job that doesn't use your strengths and hold your attention.

What Have You Learned at Work?

The life so short, the craft so long to learn.

Hippocrates
Aphorisms

BEGIN THE PROCESS of examining yourself and your passions by taking a solid look at your tangible skills and accomplishments.

Make a list of everything you've learned how to do at work. For the moment, don't worry about what might be salable, what you like, what you think you're particularly good at. For now, you're doing a simple inventory. What do you know how to do?

Sometimes we love certain things we do in our jobs that aren't really part of our job descriptions. Somebody once said that the problem with many workers is that they "do the wrong things right, rather than the right things wrong." Maybe you really love writing the monthly articles you do for the company newsletter—if the truth be told, a lot more than running your own department's weekly staff meeting. Maybe you've learned a lot about computers doing your budget spreadsheets, and you'd like to learn more—if only you didn't have all that accounting work to do.

This is the time to figure out what really excites you, what really engages you about your work. Think carefully about what you've actually done at work, not just what your job title said you were supposed to do.

Here are a few generic business skills to get you started. You'll need to add specific skills from your own profession; for example:

- If you're a mechanic, what equipment can you fix and maintain?
- If you're in a computer job, which computers have you used, what languages can you program in, what special tools (e.g., CASE methods, object-oriented programming) have you mastered?
- If you're a hospital technician, what pieces of diagnostic equipment have you learned how to use?
- If you're a graphic artist, what media can you work with, what desktop publishing or other computer tools (e.g., Adobe Illustrator, Aldus Freehand, Corel Draw) do you know how to use?

An Inventory:
What Have You Learned at Work?

Money Skills

- ❏ Accounting
- ❏ Bookkeeping
- ❏ Budgeting
- ❏ Projecting
- ❏ Purchasing
- ❏ Using computer tools (e.g., spreadsheet packages)
- ❏ Using other business machines (checkwriters, etc.)
- ❏ Knowledge of investments
- ❏ Knowledge of tax forms and laws
- ❏ Knowledge of banking regulations and procedures

Administrative/Secretarial Skills

- ❏ Telephone skills (reception, voicemail)
- ❏ Using copy machine
- ❏ Using computer tools (e.g., word processing, electronic mail)
- ❏ Using other office equipment (e.g., FAX, binding equipment)
- ❏ Taking shorthand or dictation
- ❏ Filing
- ❏ Scheduling temporary services
- ❏ Managing other people's calendars

Sales and Marketing Skills

- ❏ Generating leads
- ❏ Qualifying leads
- ❏ Developing promotional campaigns
- ❏ Developing marketing communication materials
- ❏ Pricing
- ❏ Negotiating
- ❏ Closing
- ❏ Doing competitive analyses
- ❏ Telemarketing
- ❏ Doing customer relations

- ❏ Providing technical support
- ❏ Managing trade shows

Writing and Editing Skills

- ❏ Researching
- ❏ Writing technical material
- ❏ Writing sales material
- ❏ Rewriting
- ❏ Copyediting
- ❏ Proofreading
- ❏ Indexing

Management Skills

- ❏ Hiring and firing staff
- ❏ Motivating, leading, and coaching staff
- ❏ Evaluating and developing staff
- ❏ Building team loyalty
- ❏ Directing activities
- ❏ Delegating responsibilities
- ❏ Negotiating
- ❏ Scheduling
- ❏ Planning short-term activities
- ❏ Planning long-term activities

Manufacturing Skills

- ❏ Assembling
- ❏ Soldering
- ❏ Wiring
- ❏ Fabricating
- ❏ Shipping and receiving
- ❏ Operating test equipment
- ❏ Doing quality assurance
- ❏ Expediting
- ❏ Troubleshooting
- ❏ Doing inventory management
- ❏ Managing materials
- ❏ Dealing with vendors

Maintenance Skills

- ❏ Maintaining equipment
- ❏ Diagnosing equipment problems
- ❏ Doing mechanical, electrical, and plumbing work
- ❏ Making other equipment repairs
- ❏ Doing physical plant repairs
- ❏ Wiring offices
- ❏ Retooling
- ❏ Managing warranties and service contracts
- ❏ Dealing with preventive maintenance by contractors
- ❏ Dealing with HVAC (heating, ventilation, air conditioning) contractors
- ❏ Dealing with other contractors
- ❏ Maintaining and monitoring safety records
- ❏ Dealing with government inspections (elevator safety, etc.)

Add skills for your own field:

_____

_____

_____

_____

_____

_____

_____

_____

_____

_____

What Have You Learned Outside Work?

I'll do, I'll do, and I'll do.

William Shakespeare
Macbeth

MAKE A LIST OF SKILLS you've accumulated from your life outside the office. These come from many different worlds—home, sports, volunteer activities, even your childhood. This list is particularly important if you're just starting out, if you're making a career change, or if you're returning to work after an absence (for example, while raising children).

You'll be amazed at how important this list may be to your future happiness. Just because nobody paid you to learn these skills doesn't make them less important. In fact, that may make them more important. This list may better represent the things you really love to do, the things you'd do—and did—for free.

Everything you know how to do is important. Everything you've learned can translate into a job-related skill—if you work hard enough to make it happen. For example, if you want to move into a management role in a computer software company, the budget experience you gained managing your company's softball league might be almost as important as the specific programming languages you've mastered.

Imagine combining the work skills you've mastered with the recreational interests that absorb you! Consider somebody who knows computers but whose passion is flowers—someone who spends every weekend growing and pruning and transplanting. Think about computerizing operations at a garden supply chain! A match made in heaven!

On the next few pages, I've given you a start on a list, but you'll have to supplement it with the activities and terminology that you know. Every sport and hobby has its own set of skills. Maybe you don't think of them as being transferable. But you might be surprised.

An Inventory: What Have You Learned Outside Work?

Home Skills

- ❏ Cleaning
- ❏ Cooking
- ❏ Painting
- ❏ Tiling
- ❏ Wallpapering
- ❏ Carpentry
- ❏ Doing regular house maintenance (fuses, filters, etc.)
- ❏ Maintaining and repairing home equipment
- ❏ Gardening
- ❏ Shopping
- ❏ Farming
- ❏ Hiring and supervising contractors
- ❏ Organizing special activities (parties, etc.)
- ❏ Dealing with car maintenance and repair
- ❏ Organizing and delegating family responsibilities

Nurturing Skills

- ❏ Child care
- ❏ Elder care
- ❏ Pet care and training
- ❏ Teaching (volunteering in schools, church, temple)
- ❏ Hospital or hospice work (e.g., candy striper)

Money Skills

- ❏ Budgeting
- ❏ Handling bank, trust, and retirement accounts
- ❏ Making investments
- ❏ Buying and monitoring insurance
- ❏ Negotiating
- ❏ Maintaining warranties and other records

Intellectual Skills

- ❏ Reading (Do you like to read? What types of books?)
- ❏ Writing (fiction, nonfiction, technical, business?)
- ❏ Language skills (Which do you speak? Read?)
- ❏ Collecting and appreciating art
- ❏ Anything else you've taken courses in

Hobby/Sport Skills

- ❏ Collecting and valuing coins, stamps, and other collectibles
- ❏ Adventures (e.g., rock-climbing, spelunking)
- ❏ Travel (Have you lived in other countries?)
- ❏ Sports (Which sports do you love? Which can you play well?)
- ❏ Games (Which games do you love? Which can you play well?)
- ❏ Music (Which instruments do you love? Which can you play well?)
- ❏ Machinery (e.g., power tools, ham radio) (Which can you use? Repair?)
- ❏ Fixing and customizing cars
- ❏ Collecting rocks, flowers, mushrooms

Artistic Skills

- ❏ Drawing
- ❏ Painting
- ❏ Sculpting
- ❏ Doing embroidery, knitting, etc.
- ❏ Photography

Electronic Skills

- ❏ Using or programming home computers
- ❏ Programming VCRs
- ❏ Selecting and maintaining stereo equipment

Add your own skills:

_____

_____

_____

_____

Mix Business with Pleasure

Perfect freedom is reserved for the man who lives by his own work,
and in that work does what he wants to do.

R.G. Collingwood
Speculum Mentis

WHEN YOU'RE THINKING about what you can do—at work and out-side it—don't leave anything out. Cast yourself back in time, and consider all the odd jobs, hobbies, athletic pursuits, and social activities that might have given you skills of any kind.

As more and more people discover the joys of exercise, you may find that your college job managing the indoor athletic building and running training classes for the sports teams can be parlayed into a job you love at your town's new exercise center.

As the number of two-working-parent families increases, you may find that your cook-ing experience can translate into a small business opportunity packaging ready-to-eat meals that can be brought home from local day care centers.

You may wonder why on earth your employers would care that you collect stamps or know how to ice skate. If you're applying for a banking job, chances are they won't. But you're not at the stage yet where you're winnowing down and eliminating. Right now, you're being as inclusive as possible. You're figuring out what you know and what you've accumulated. Maybe you'll end up doing budgeting for a stamp collecting organization. Maybe you'll decide to start a skating clinic at your local rink. The point is, you *don't* know yet.

About ten years ago, Bill Clark, the vice-president of a major international bank, had an insight. Bill played backgammon and chess in his spare time, and he wondered if the ability to play these games at a world-class level might be transferable to the world of investments. As an experiment, he hired several young players who had been making their livings playing and betting on backgammon and chess. Clark gave them training in international currency trading, and they became a tremendous success. It turned out that the same ability to focus on a game under pressure, to see many moves ahead, and to put poor decisions immediately behind them served these players well in the cha-otic, pressure-filled world of international currency exchange. Several of Clark's prote-gees, who once lived on the poverty line, making do from one match to the next, have gone on to make millions for their employers, their clients, and themselves.

What Kind of Person Are You?

The longest journey is the journey inward.

Dag Hammarskjöld

MAKE A LIST of your personal attributes—not what you've done, but how you've done it. Are you a creative force, or are you more comfortable following someone else's direction? Are you flexible enough to change direction in the middle of a project? Are you superb at listing all the tasks and eventualities that might arise? Think long and hard about *who* you are before you resolve on *what* you should work at.

The poet Gerald Manley Hopkins, who made up so many odd and expressive words, invented a wonderful verb, "to selve," which means to be yourself. If you can be yourself—if you can express the type of person you are—in your work, you'll have a job you'll truly love.

An Inventory:
What Kind of Person Are You?

This list is only a start. Add to it the qualities you value and you see in yourself.

Personal Qualities

❏ Energy
❏ Drive
❏ Charisma
❏ Even temperament
❏ Ability to lead
❏ Ability to follow
❏ Stick-to-it-iveness, persistence
❏ Perseverance, endurance
❏ Humor and ability to entertain
❏ Creativity and imagination
❏ Ability to make a decision
❏ Initiative
❏ Bravery and willingness to take risks
❏ Flexibility
❏ Frugality
❏ Loyalty
❏ Confidence
❏ Reliability
❏ Integrity and honesty
❏ Efficiency
❏ Ability to follow rules, procedures, chain of command
❏ Ability to think fast on feet
❏ Organization
❏ Time management
❏ Ability to be a self starter
❏ Tendency to be methodical
❏ Ability to look at all sides of a situation

People Skills

❏ Patience (with different types of people and work styles)
❏ Communication (one-to-one, small groups, large groups)

- ❏ Training and coaching
- ❏ Facilitation and mediation
- ❏ Supervision and evaluation
- ❏ Discipline
- ❏ Ability to inspire, motivate, engage, and encourage
- ❏ Ability to include and support others
- ❏ Listening
- ❏ Delegation
- ❏ Persuasion
- ❏ Negotiation
- ❏ Ability to work well by self
- ❏ Ability to work well with peers
- ❏ Ability to work well with management
- ❏ Ability to work well with subordinates
- ❏ Ability to work well with young children
- ❏ Ability to work well with teenagers
- ❏ Ability to work well with elderly people
- ❏ Ability to work well with sick people

Add your own special qualities:

_____

_____

_____

_____

_____

_____

_____

_____

What Are Your Natural Talents?

First of all, try to forget that you have ever heard of the concept of intelligence as a single property of the human mind; or of that instrument called the intelligence test, which purports to measure intelligence once and for all. Second of all, cast your mind widely about the world and think of all the roles or "end states"— vocational and avocational—that have been prized by cultures during various eras. Consider, for example, hunters, fishermen, farmers, shamans, religious leaders, psychiatrists, military leaders, civil leaders, athletes, artists, musicians, poets, parents, and scientists.

Howard Gardner
Frames of Mind

DIFFERENT PEOPLE have different innate talents, inclinations, and interests. Traditionally, our Western systems of education and human development have measured intelligence as a single entity. In *Frames of Mind*, Howard Gardner explores the "theory of multiple intelligences," a way of assessing and appreciating levels of competence in skills that range far more widely than those measured by typical intelligence tests. Gardner defines seven main "intelligences," shown on the facing page.

Gardner points out that each of these intelligences has its own pattern of development and its own distinct neurological pattern. Different intelligences are cultivated in distinct ways by different cultures. Gardner also leaves open the possibility of many other types of intelligences as well.

An innate bent for one area of life does not necessarily imply that you must spend your life carrying out its dictates. Students who have a natural talent for math or music quite often land happily in jobs that challenge them to develop writing or management skills that do not come naturally. And gifted writers sometimes find themselves in medicine or computer science, where they struggle to catch up, but love the attempt. Knowing your strengths and your own particular "intelligences" doesn't force you to nurture them. But it gives you valuable information in your quest for work that suits both your talents and your passions.

Seven Distinct Intelligences

Linguistic — Characterizes many writers, debaters, and those who learn foreign languages with ease.

Musical — Characterizes those who compose or perform music.

Logical-Mathematical — Characterizes mathematicians, scientists, and logicians.

Spatial — Characterizes chess players, navigators, artists, and certain types of scientists.

Bodily-Kinesthetic — Characterizes dancers, athletes, and certain types of inventors.

Intrapersonal — Characterizes those who have a powerful and independent understanding of their own emotional life: certain types of writers and poets, therapists, and wise elders.

Interpersonal — Characterizes those who notice and empathize with other individuals: political and religious leaders, teachers, and those in the helping professions.

With the permission of the Teachers' Curriculum Institute (TCI) of Palo Alto, California, we've included a brief test designed for teachers to use with their students. Your responses to this test may help give you at least an initial glimpse at what your true "intelligences" might be.

Read each statement. If it expresses some characteristic of yours and sounds true for the most part, mark down a "T." If it doesn't, mark an "F." If the statement is sometimes true, sometimes false, leave it blank.

What Is Your Own Type of Intelligence?

1. __ I'd rather draw a map than give someone verbal directions.
2. __ If I am angry or happy, I usually know exactly why.
3. __ I can play (or used to play) a musical instrument.
4. __ I can associate music with my moods.
5. __ I can add or multiply quickly in my head.
6. __ I can help a friend sort out strong feelings because I successfully dealt with similar feelings myself.
7. __ I like to work with calculators and computers.
8. __ I pick up new dance steps fast.
9. __ It's easy for me to say what I think in an argument or debate.
10. __ I enjoy a good lecture, speech, or sermon.
11. __ I always know north from south no matter where I am.
12. __ I like to gather together groups of people for parties or special events.
13. __ Life seems empty without music.
14. __ I always understand the drawings that come with new gadgets or appliances.
15. __ I like to work puzzles and play games.
16. __ Learning to ride a bike (or skates) was easy.
17. __ I am irritated when I hear an argument or statement that sounds illogical.
18. __ I can convince others to follow my plans.
19. __ My sense of balance and coordination is good.
20. __ I often see patterns and relationships between numbers faster and easier than others.
21. __ I enjoy building models (or sculpting).
22. __ I'm good at finding the fine points of word meanings.
23. __ I can look at an object one way and see it turned sideways or backwards just as easily.
24. __ I often connect a piece of music with some event in my life.
25. __ I like to work with numbers and figures.
26. __ I like to sit quietly and reflect on my inner feelings.
27. __ Just looking at shapes of buildings and structures pleases me.
28. __ I like to hum, whistle and sing in the shower or when I'm alone.
29. __ I'm good at athletics.
30. __ I enjoy writing detailed letters to friends.
31. __ I'm usually aware of the expression on my face.
32. __ I'm sensitive to the expressions on other people's faces.
33. __ I stay "in touch" with my moods. I have no trouble identifying them.
34. __ I am sensitive to the moods of others.
35. __ I have a good sense of what others think of me.

Scoring Sheet

Circle each item which you marked as T for true. Add your totals. A total of four in any of the categories indicates strong ability.

A.	B.	C	D	E	F	G.
9	5	1	8	3	2	12
10	7	11	16	4	6	18
17	15	14	19	13	26	32
22	20	23	21	24	31	34
30	25	27	29	28	33	35

Totals: ____   ____   ____   ____   ____   ____   ____

A = Linguistic Intelligence

B = Logical-Mathematical Intelligence

C = Spatial Intelligence

D = Bodily-Kinesthetic Intelligence

E = Musical Intelligence

F = Intrapersonal Intelligence

G = Interpersonal Intelligence

How Do Others See You?

Ah wad some power the giftie gie us
To see oursels as others see us!

Robert Burns
To a Mouse

SOME PEOPLE FIND it hard to take a good look at themselves and figure out who they are and where they should be going. If you're mired down in decision-making about what career is right for you, you may need a push from a friend or a professional. First, turn to those who know you best.

Phyllis Jorgensen was a secretary interested in making a career move. She asked Frank, a former boss who had become the comptroller of a rival company, his opinion about the right job for her. He told her he thought she belonged in training. "Why do you say that?" she asked, surprised because she'd never worked in the training field. Frank recounted a story of a project she'd done that had impressed him.

The computer company for which they'd worked wanted to reduce the cost of office supplies. Phyllis undertook to figure out how her department could save money on supplies. She made some calls, visited the new local discount office supply stores, as well as the traditional suppliers, discussed with them their various discount programs for large purchasers, their delivery policies, and other variables, and came up with a recommendation for using a new supplier based on the research she'd done. She made up some simple overhead slides showing the different prices and the issues that had gone into her recommendation. At the next departmental meeting she made a 10-minute presentation.

Frank told Phyllis that he dealt with senior executives all the time and her presentation compared favorably with the best he'd seen. It was simple, it told all the facts, it used clear visuals, and it made a recommendation that was sane and easy to implement. She was flabbergasted. "But that was fun," she told me later, "It wasn't even work!"

I was reminded of the old saying, "If it were easy, we wouldn't call it work, would we?" But, in fact, sometimes it is easy. There's no law that we can't do work we're good at, work we'll love.

The most important voice is your own. But, sometimes other people are able to appreciate certain qualities you may not recognize or value in yourself—qualities that may help you select a career or find a job that's right for you.

An Exercise in Figuring Out
How Others See You

Interview about half a dozen people—whether they are friends, family, coworkers, or current or former bosses—people who know you well and care about you. I've sometimes said that the opposite of dishonesty isn't honesty, it's brutal honesty. We're not looking for brutal here. We're looking for people who will be honest, as well as compassionate and common-sensical.

Ask your carefully selected subjects three questions:

1. What do you think my greatest strengths are?
2. What do you think my greatest weaknesses are?
3. If you were picking a job for me, what would you pick? What do you think I'd be really terrific at?

You'll be surprised at how effective this exercise can be. You'll often get answers that surprise you but may also open your eyes to new and apt possibilities.

Look Carefully at the World of Work

No man is born into the world, whose work
is not born with him; there is always work,
And tools to work withal, for those who will.

James Russell Lowell
A Glance Behind the Curtain

MOST PEOPLE DON'T KNOW how to go about picking a career that suits their skills, interests, and personality. Many are confused and frustrated with their attempts to find or change jobs. Maybe you're making a career choice for the first time. Or maybe you've made a poor choice and you'd like to try again.

I tell the people I counsel to deal from a full deck. What does that mean? Most people make their choice of a career from very few options—maybe four or five choices. This just doesn't make sense. If you go to eat at a restaurant that offers only four or five items on its menu, you'll probably feel cheated. If you try to pick a pair of aces from a deck containing only ten cards, you'll be unlikely to succeed. You've got to give yourself enough scope, enough information.

Although I don't recommend that you go straight for the trendy jobs, I do think it's important for you to know how wide the world of work really is these days. There are thousands of different types of jobs out there. Many of them—environmental technicians, paralegals, and physicians assistants—may not have existed the last time you looked around for a career or a job. Some might not even be listed in books of career opportunities. Before telephone company deregulation, there were no Baby Bells. Now there are thousands of jobs in these companies. Until recently, health care cost containment was an abstract goal. Now, with utilization review, insurance reimbursement for hospital procedures is more closely regulated, creating many new jobs in every hospital and insurance company in the United States. Biotechnology didn't exist ten years ago. Now, careers and fortunes are made here. No wonder we're confused.

Before you start churning the waters, trying to find the same kind of job you have now, give yourself the luxury of some time to learn what's out there. Reading the want ads and the business pages is a good way to find out what kinds of jobs exist. If something sounds appealing, write it down. For now, don't try to psych out whether you're qualified or whether there are jobs available in your area. Just get the lay of the land.

What do You Want from the Want Ads?

Although many job hunters go first to the want ads, it's a sad fact that only about five percent of jobs are found through all published openings—newspaper ads, trade journals, job opportunity bulletin boards, online services, etc. So, don't put all your hopes in the Sunday paper.

Although many people overestimate the usefulness of the want ads in actually finding a job, most also underestimate the more general informational benefits of reading these ads. Finding a specific job is only one reason to read the want ads. Here are some others:

- The want ads may help you find new career paths to explore—there may be ads for jobs you never knew existed.
- They may give you clues about job titles—you may know what you want to do, but not what it's called these days.
- They may tell you which companies are growing and hiring—a company may need you, and not even know it yet!
- They may help you find out which companies are in the geographical or functional area where you think you want to work.
- They may give you contact names within companies—and maybe a start on networking with somebody who might be helpful in your own job search.
- They may reveal salary information—less true these days, but still a possibility.

Old Fields, New Jobs

U.S. News and World Report (October 26, 1992) identified "hot tracks" in 20 traditional professions—jobs that might not appear in your job directory or jobs that, because of economic conditions or other trends, are making a comeback.

Accounting	Environmental accountant
Computers	Network administrator
Consulting	Outplacement consultant
Education	Special-education teacher
Engineering	Civil engineer
Environment	Toxicologist
Finance	Investment professional
Food Service	Restaurant site selector
Health Care	Nurse practitioner
Human Resources	Training manager
Insurance	Actuary
Law	Intellectual property lawyer
Manufacturing	Chief information officer
Medicine	Family physician
Nonprofits	Member services director
Office Administration	Technical administrative assistant
Publishing	Electronic publishing specialist
Retailing	Merchandise manager
Science Research	Computational chemist
Telecommunications	Wireless specialist

Fine-Tune Your Targets

There is a passion for hunting something deeply implanted in the human breast.

Charles Dickens
Oliver Twist

YOU'VE DONE YOUR HOMEWORK. You've figured out what gets you motivated and unmotivated, you've analyzed your skills, you've dreamed a dream or two, and you've talked to some people who have realized the dreams you've been dreaming for yourself. You've also done some research into what kinds of jobs are out there. Now, you're ready to define and find that new job or career. How?

Here's an analogy for you. Hunt for a job the way you'd hunt for wild game in the woods. This may be a politically incorrect analogy, but it has the appropriately hair-raising qualities of our job search. The way *not* to search in the woods for game is to pick up a gun and wander aimlessly, peering behind trees, saying "There's nothing here. Oh, there's nothing here either," making a lot of noise and trying not to get hopelessly lost and starve to death. Real hunters—and expert job-hunters—have a strategy. They understand the terrain and they know what the target looks like. They know the best hunting tools and how to use them. They know when it's time to hunt, and when it's better to quit and try again another day.

Even if you've never aimed a gun or an arrow, you know it's got to be easier to hit a target if you know what that target looks like. If you stumble into your ideal job, how will you know it?

There are three distinct types of targets you need to identify:

* Function—What specific job do you want to do?
* Industry or industry-segment—In what industry, or company, can you expect to find that job, or do you want to find that job?
* Geography—Where is this industry, or company, geographically?

Think of these targets as windows on the world of work. The wider you open the windows, the more opportunities you'll see. If you'll accept any job in any industry anywhere in the United States, I'll find a job for you tomorrow. But do you want to be unloading building supplies in Las Vegas? Usually, you'll want to close the window, at least a little, to narrow your search to a particular type of job in a particular area.

Focus, but Be Flexible

"The time has come," the Walrus said,
"To talk of many things:"

Lewis Carroll
Through the Looking-Glass

BE FOCUSED with your job targets, but try not to narrow your initial search too much. If you're determined to be a lion tamer in a circus in a mountain state, you're likely to be jobless for some time to come. If you're keen on selling ice fishing supplies, you're unlikely to find opportunities in Key West. If you want to be a career diplomat, there are only so many State Departments available. Some combinations are pretty obvious. But usually, it's a lot harder, and you'll have to do your homework.

Don't ever decide that there's only one job in the world that's right for you. Be clear about your skills and interests, but try to be flexible about how and where you'll apply them. Here's one example. Suppose you want a job in publishing. Maybe you have some graphics experience using Macintosh computers. Your ideal fit? Working in the graphics department of a publishing house. But, if there are no perfect jobs out there, you might decide that your interest in publishing is paramount and aim for any available publishing jobs you're qualified for—editorial assistant, copyeditor, sales and marketing support.

On the other hand, you might decide that, for now, you want to use your graphics experience, even outside the publishing business. Lots of organizations have small desktop publishing groups. Consider working for a small business—a product manufacturer or a consulting company—that's trying to cut ad agency and typesetter costs by generating product ads, fliers, and newsletters inhouse.

How Do You Feel About Job Hunting?

Let me assert my firm belief that the only thing
we have to fear is fear itself.

Franklin Delano Roosevelt
First Inaugural Address, 1933

LOOKING FOR A JOB is a tough process, and it's no wonder so many of us settle for something less than the ideal. The fact is, most people would rather get their teeth drilled than look for a job. It's hard work—tiring, frustrating, and often demoralizing. We hate rejection, an inevitable part of the process for most of us. And it's hard to get really good at job hunting because we get so little feedback about our performance. As a result, too many people stay in jobs they don't like. When they're forced to look for a job, they tend to take the first job that comes along—anything to stop the pain of looking!

Unfortunately, job hunting often is not an optional activity. Many people—especially these days—are cast unwillingly into the job market. In an 18-month period between 1990 and 1992, 1.9 million jobs were eliminated, and 25 percent of the work force (20 million people) were unemployed during some part of that period. It's estimated that the top 500 companies in the United States will be eliminating another 4 million jobs by the year 2000. And this recession is, more than any other we've seen recently, a white-collar one. The rate of unemployment among college educated workers is expected to be close to 10 percent by 1998. (Statistics from *U.S. News and World Report*, January 13, 1992.)

The statistics make it more necessary to find jobs—and often to switch careers—than ever before. More and more people are switching career paths—some because jobs aren't available in their own fields anymore, and some to find greater job satisfaction. Statistics show that, on average, people keep their jobs five to six years (in some industries and job functions, the average is only two to three years), so most of us will switch jobs at least eight times during our working lives, and will have three or four distinct careers.

You're unlikely to land a job you love without fighting to find that job. Try to overcome your fears and anxieties about job hunting by focusing on the reason you're hunting—not to make the pain stop, but to find the place where you can be your best self.

What's Stopping You?

*To fear is one thing. To let fear grab you by the tail
and swing you around is another.*

Katherine Patterson
Jacob Have I Loved You

CAN YOU MAKE your dreams come true? What's stopping you from going out and living up to your best imaginings? For most of us, fear stops us from being all we can be.

Emotions matter more than most of us realize. If emotions didn't enter into your work life, you'd be content to do just about any job, day after day, as long as it paid well. But you know that, for most people, that's not the case. An important first step in overcoming our fears and living up to our dreams, is to admit that emotions do influence us, and sometimes even overwhelm us. If you acknowledge your feelings, you'll be better able to understand why you do what you do—and how you can do better.

A lot of people don't like dealing with their emotions, I don't think you need to be psychoanalyzed before you can write your resumé or go to work. But I do think that all of us need to feel as well as act. People who do one at the expense of the other—either way—aren't going to do very well.

I tend to be a pretty pragmatic psychologist. Even in my work with war veterans, I listen, I console, I admit the terrible pain inflicted upon them and the difficulty of putting it behind them. But I force them to try. While I'm listening to them, I'm also saying things like, "I think it might be a good idea to get you some clean clothes and a shave," or "We'll talk about this more after you register for school." I don't want them to submerge their feelings. I do want them to put these feelings aside for the moment. I want them to understand that they're going to feel better if they can get their lives moving again.

It's always a mix. With vets and other people who may be mired down in their feelings, I encourage them to put those feelings aside and make some tangible progress in their lives. With clean clothes, a job, and a decent meal, they're going to feel better, even with all the unresolved horror in their backgrounds. With people who don't think they have time for feelings, I take a different route. I encourage them to take a little time to understand themselves—particularly if they're trying to transform themselves in some way—from unsuccessful to successful, from student to worker, from sad worker to happy worker, from follower to leader.

There will be a lot of time to act. Take just a little time to try to understand who you are, what motivates you, and why you act the way you do. You'll find yourself in a much better position to make the right moves.

Why Are You Afraid?

No passion so effectually robs the mind of all its powers
of acting and reasoning as fear.

Edmund Burke

IT'S FRIGHTENING to deal with issues like choosing a career, looking for a job, and trying to excel in our jobs. Millions of people stay in jobs they can't stand because the only thing worse than doing their jobs is looking for another one. Why are we afraid, and what difference does it make?

Consider for a moment where we all come from. Back when our ancestors were cave men and women, along came the saber-toothed tiger to make their day. The cave folk reacted in one of three ways: First, there were those who admired Ol' Saber and said, in effect (remember, this is pre-speech), "Nice kitty." Those folks dropped out of the gene pool early, so not many of us are related to them. Then, there were the fighters. These folks saw a tiger and stood their ground. Some actually survived their folly. Finally, there were what I'll call the flighters. These folks (there are still a lot of them around today, for obvious reasons) saw a tiger and said, "Tiger! Problem! Later!" They lived to fight, or flee, another day.

The fight or flight reaction, however primordial, still dominates our emotional lives. When we see a threat—be it a tiger, a truck swerving towards us, or an interview with Personnel—our bodies react with adrenalin. We become fearful, anxious, and angry. Everything we feel is heightened.

That fear and anxiety affects us. However civilized we've become, however well we hide the emotions that lurk beneath the surface, the fear is there and it works against us. Suppose I told you I'd pay you $10 to walk along a plank of wood that I'd placed on the floor. It's six inches across and ten feet long. No problem. Anybody can do it. Easy ten bucks. Now, suppose I stretch the same plank between two buildings, say 100 feet up. This time, I'll offer you $100—maybe even $1000. Same plank, same distance. Could you do it? I'll bet you couldn't. Now, there's fear. You're breathing hard, your knees are clicking together. Your fear is going to overcome your confidence.

This is the kind of thing that happens when you think about switching careers and hunting for a job. You're afraid. The fear keeps you from deciding to leave a job you hate. The fear forces you to accept the first job that comes along. The fear keeps you from trying to switch careers. You need to realize that you're dealing with scary stuff. Your emotions are going to cut down on your ability to concentrate and excel.

You can't make fear or anger or any other emotion go away completely. But you can learn to put your feelings aside for a time while you get on with the task at hand.

Measure the Stress You Feel

Change is stressful, and changes in our jobs can be just as stressful as other dramatic and difficult life events. In the famous Holmes-Rahe Life Event-Stress Scale,[8] Thomas H. Holmes and R.H. Rahe measured the relative impact of various stressful events in our lives. Holmes and Rahe predicted that if your total "stress score" for a 12-month period is 300 or more, you run a major risk of developing some kind of illness, as a consequence of the stress, within the next year. Of course, your own situation, and the way you're able to adjust to stressful situations ultimately determines the particular impact changes will have on your life and health.

We've included the scale on the facing page and highlighted the job-related events. Note that being fired ranks just beneath death of a spouse, divorce, separation, jail term, death of a close family member, personal injury or illness, and marriage.

Scale reprinted with permission from Holmes, T.H. and Rahe, R.H.: "The Social Readjustment Rating Scale," from Journal of Psychosomatic Research, *11:3; 1967, Pergamon Press Ltd, Oxford, England.*

Life Event-Stress Scale

Rank	Life Event	Value	Your Score
1	Death of spouse	100	_____
2	Divorce	73	_____
3	Marital separation	65	_____
4	Jail term	63	_____
5	Death of a close family member	63	_____
6	Personal injury or illness	53	_____
7	Marriage	50	_____
8	*Fired at work*	47	_____
9	Marital reconciliation	45	_____
10	*Retirement*	45	_____
11	Change in health of family member	44	_____
12	Pregnancy	40	_____
13	Sexual difficulties	39	_____
14	Gain of new family member	39	_____
15	*Business adjustment (merger, bankruptcy, etc.)*	39	_____
16	Change in financial status	38	_____
17	Death of close friend	37	_____
18	*Change to different line of work*	36	_____
19	Change in number of arguments with spouse	35	_____
20	Mortgage or loan over $100,000*	31	_____
21	Foreclosure of mortgage or loan	30	_____
22	*Change in responsibilities at work*	29	_____
23	Son or daughter leaving home	29	_____
24	Trouble with in-laws	29	_____
25	Outstanding personal achievement	28	_____
26	Spouse beginning or stopping work	26	_____
27	Beginning or ending school	26	_____
28	Change in living conditions	25	_____
29	Revision of personal habits	24	_____
30	*Trouble with boss*	23	_____
31	*Change in work hours or conditions*	20	_____
32	Change in residence	20	_____
33	Change in schools	20	_____
34	Change in recreation	19	_____
35	Change in church activities	19	_____
36	Change in social activities	18	_____
37	Mortgage or loan less than $100,000*	17	_____
38	Change in sleeping habits	16	_____
39	Change in number of family get-togethers	15	_____
40	Change in eating habits	15	_____
41	Vacation	13	_____
42	Christmas	12	_____
43	Minor violations of the law	11	_____
		Total	_____

* These were $10,000 in the original scale. We've adjusted for inflation.

Say No to Negative Messages

He who will teach the child to doubt
The rotting grave shall ne'er get out.

William Blake
Auguries of Innocence

WE HEAR A LOT of negative messages every day. Our parents, spouses, children, and teachers may be asking too much of us—making us feel like a failure for not meeting their every need. Our bosses are telling us what we do wrong—never what we do right. The news is full of bad, sad stories.

One reason job hunting is so hard is that it's usually just one negative message after another. Everybody hates to get rejected. Human nature being what it is, we tend to learn after several rejections to shy away from whatever it was that rejected us. But that's hardly a way to succeed in our job hunt. Hard as it is, the more we're rejected, the more we have to keep plugging.

In a job hunt, no matter how qualified you may be, you're going to get rejected a lot. There may not be enough jobs in your industry or area. There may not be a good fit between you and the company you'd like to work at. *You need to try to separate the rejection of you, the job applicant, from the rejection of you, the person.* You need to treat rejection as par for the course, part of the process. I tell the people I counsel that if they're not getting rejected enough, they're not looking enough and trying enough.

For many of us, the worst obstacles to finding the right job, and finding satisfaction at work, are the negative messages that swirl around whenever we try something new:

> That's not the way it's done.
> Don't make waves.
> It won't work.
> It's been tried.

On top of these messages from the outside world are those we find inside ourselves:

> I was never good at this.
> I can't stand up and say that.
> I haven't learned how to do that.

Hearing these messages over and over again makes us tired, depressed, and doubtful about our real worth.

An Exercise in Beating Negative Messages

1. Try to monitor your own thinking for a month or so. While you're dreaming of success, or fretting about your lack of it, what kinds of thoughts cross your mind? Some of them are positive—for example:

   > That was a really good idea I had.

   > I'm smarter than most people; I ought to be able to become a manager.

   Some of them are negative—for example:

   > I'm not aggressive enough.

   > I'm never going to make a big success in the adventure/travel business.

   Slow down and record these thoughts in the notebook you started in an earlier exercise—both the positive and the negative.

2. At the end of the month, look at the positive messages and resolve to focus on these messages. They'll help you stay motivated by your own feelings of success.

3. Now look at the negative messages and ask yourself:

   > Do I really believe this negative message?

   > Where did I pick up this message? From whom?

   > What can I do to disprove this message?

   The next time a negative thought crosses your mind, interrupt that thought and question its logic. Turn to a positive thought instead.

4. For special encouragement, think about the words of Margaret Chase Smith, former Senator from Maine. Most of us are swayed and discouraged by negative messages, but a few, like Senator Smith, have unquenchable spirits that actually thrive on the challenge. She said:

   > *When people keep telling you that you can't do a thing, you kind of like to try it.*

We All Fear Failure

If you want to conquer fear, don't sit at home and think about it. Go out and get busy.

Dale Carnegie

JUST ABOUT EVERYBODY is afraid of failure. If we don't perform up to the standards we've set for ourselves—or others have set for us—we risk disappointment, disapproval, humiliation, or even shame. Some people can't bear to take risks; they don't know what's on the other side of the door, so they won't open it. Some people are perfectionists; they'd rather not do anything than do something less than their best.

How does fear of failure translate into the quest for a job you love? Searching for the right career, looking for a new job, and trying out new activities at work are inherently risk-taking pursuits. So, what's the solution? Don't respond to any ads. You might get rejected. Don't go to any interviews. They might not like you. Don't accept any offers. You might not like the job.

A more realistic way of coping with fear of failure is to deal with it head-on. Think about this as you're going into an interview you've been dreading: What's the worst that can happen? You won't be offered the job. Suppose they embarrass and insult you? Would you really want to work for such people? If it gets really bad, remember that your feet aren't stapled to the floor. You *can* get up and leave! The interview won't bring the end of the world as we know it.

It's hard to get over our very natural fear of failure. We've had a lot of practice. And we're not going to turn things around completely. But, if we keep taking risks, we'll get a little braver and more confident every day. Remember, you can't possibly know if you're going to get a job—or like that job—unless you take a chance on finding out.

An Exercise in Managing Your Fears

1. What is it, right now, that you are feeling about finding a new career? Don't get intellectual. The purpose is to identify and deal with feelings, not abstract concepts.

2. Think as negative as you like, for now anyway. If you go to this interview, call this person, or don't get this job, what's the worst that can happen? Will you die? Will you be publicly ostracized? Will you lose your marriage? Will you lose the job you have now? Will you make less money? Will your family starve? Will you not get that new job? Will your self-esteem suffer?

   Remember that this worst-case exercise is probably just that—an exercise. It's very unlikely that your dire imaginings will turn into reality.

3. Now, decide what you'd do if your imaginings did come true. Your solution may not be a wholly satisfactory one. But you may find it reassuring just to know that you *do* have a plan for that very unlikely worst-case scenario.

4. What positive outcome is possible if you take the risk you've been dreading? Will you get a new job? Will you make more money? Will you become a household word? Will your confidence increase?

5. Who has gone through this type of turmoil—whether it's a job hunt or some other crisis—and can help you deal with these feelings?

   If you ask, you'll find that friends, colleagues, and neighbors have faced just what you're facing now. They have ideas and experiences to share with you. They can help you face the fear of the unknown.

Take the Reality Test

*The knowledge of the world is only to be acquired
in the world, and not in a closet.*

Philip Dormer Stanhope, Earl of Chesterfield
Letters

DO YOU REALLY WANT to go where no one has ever gone before—and
do people really get paid for going there? It's very important to test our images of certain professions before we get too far down the road. Sometimes our glorified images don't correspond to reality. One good way to find out what a job is like is to talk to people who do that job for a living. Forget the illusions, the traditions, the folklore, the media. See how these people spend their days and nights. What you find out may turn you on, or it may turn you off. It may make you reconsider, or refine, your game plan. But it will give you information. And that's what you're after.

My old friend Charlie Rabinowitz always loved sailing and hated cold weather. After years of sticking it out in administrative jobs he hated up North, he decided to go for broke as captain of a charter boat in the Virgin Islands (average temperature 86 degrees). This sounded mighty fine. I often wondered what became of him and when I finally took a vacation down there, I looked Charlie up. I found that he'd sold the boat and was working in a video studio with no windows. I'm an observant fellow and I noticed that this was not outdoors (86 degrees, remember?). In fact, inside things were a lot like Boston.

Charlie told me that yep, the weather had been great, the boat had been great, but he couldn't stand the people who rented his boat. "They wanted me to bring them beers," he said. "They complained that I didn't have Heinekens!"

Charlie's problem was that, in all his relocation and his boat shopping, he never once talked to anyone who actually *did* the job he wanted to have. So nobody ever told him that he was going to spend a lot more time serving beers and telling people they couldn't wear high heels on deck than he would navigating around shoals and letting the wind whip through his hair.

You'll be amazed at how willing people are to share information and feelings about their jobs with people like you who are genuinely interested in their stories. Just make sure they know you're seeking information and inspiration, not a job here and now.

An Exercise in Reality Testing

Once you have settled on a particular job objective, interview several people who actually do the job you dream about. Ask them these questions—and others you care about:

About themselves:

1. How and when did you get into this field?
2. How did you prepare for this job?
3. What exactly do you do?
4. What kinds of people do you work with?
5. What is your day like (if it's possible to generalize)?

About their job and field:

1. What does your department do? How does your job fit in?
2. How are decisions made? What decisions do you make?
3. What is the best part of your job? What is the worst?
4. What other obligations (lectures, travel, teaching, social events) go along with your job?
5. What is the salary range for people in this field?
6. What kinds of changes are going on in your field/profession?
7. What kinds of problems occur in your field or organization?
8. What professional newspapers and journals do you read? What associations do you belong to?
9. What trends do you foresee in your field over the next three to five years?
10. Do you anticipate growth in your field during the next five years? In what areas?

About your own career:

1. What would my prospects be in this field?
2. Who is best-suited for this kind of job (what type of talent and personality)?
3. What skills, education, and experience would you look for in a candidate?
4. What additional training would you recommend for me?
5. What advice can you give me about finding a job in this field?
6. Who could I contact for additional information?

Make It Tangible

Nothing ever becomes real till it is experienced—even a proverb
is no proverb to you till your life has illustrated it.

John Keats,
letter to George and Georgianna Keats

SOME BOOKS ON JOBS and careers emphasize self-assessment and mental preparation so heavily that I question whether the reader will ever find the time and energy to go look for a job. Our culture's recent focus on getting in touch with our feelings sometimes borders on self-indulgence. Of course, self-assessment and dealing with emotions are important, and many of the exercises in this book ask you to look inside yourself. But, don't get bogged down. Look outside yourself too. Make some moves. Stir yourself up. Action often teaches us more than all the self-contemplation in the world.

William James put it this way: "Actions seem to follow feeling, but really action and feeling go together." In his own work as a psychologist, James found that people who coupled action with self-analysis were able to make much more rapid changes in their ways of viewing themselves and the world. Action reinforced feeling, and vice versa.

In the early 1970s, the era of public school desegregation in Boston, I worked as a team member to try to help parents deal with the realities of busing. In a series of meetings, we tried—pretty ineffectively—to explain schedules, security, and why busing was necessary. Feelings ran high. One team member suggested that we do more than talk. Some parents were asked to try out the buses. Accompanied by the same bus monitors who would travel with their children, they drove the route and saw the sights their children would encounter on their journey: the policeman on the corner, the stores and playgrounds they'd pass, the entrance to the school grounds. Then they toured the school and checked out the facilities. When we asked parents to evaluate the training and to assess whether their own feelings had changed at all, we found that the parents who had boarded the buses felt much more comfortable about their children's busing. We didn't succeed in making the process an altogether smooth and happy one. But, our experiments helped at least some parents to cope better with a difficult situation.

Because feeling and action are so closely linked, I encourage people to go beyond thinking and analyzing when they're pondering which career is right for them. Interview people who work at the jobs you dream about, go to seminars or exhibitions sponsored by professions you'd like to be a part of, try out different jobs on a volunteer basis. These are all good ways of acting on your feelings about jobs and career goals.

Experience is the Most Precious Commodity

In the business world, everyone is paid in two coins:
cash and experience. Take the experience first;
the cash will come later.

Harold Geneen

SOMETIMES, we need to make temporary financial sacrifices to gain experience in a new profession. Experience in a job you love—and will grow to love even more as you develop in it—is more precious than gold.

Tom Maloney was a foreman working first shift in an auto plant. He made a good salary, earned more with overtime, and had excellent benefits. He liked the money, but he hated his day-to-day supervisory work. When he thought carefully about his past and his future, he realized that the most challenging and enjoyable part of his work was the union side of it. He was particularly good at negotiating and at researching and understanding contract data. Tom had attended a community college, but family and financial responsibilities had intervened before he got more than an associate degree. Tom realized, though, that he had always had some interest in the law.

Now that his children were grown and his wife had gone back to work, Tom had a little financial leeway in his life. He decided that getting experience in a field he felt he could love was more important than money. It was now or never.

Tom found a federal program that let him explore his interest in law by retraining as a paralegal assistant. As time went on, he was able to learn more by taking an unpaid internship in a government office, working on labor and arbitration issues. Through that work, Tom met an attorney who specialized in worker's compensation law and who found Tom's union background valuable. Ultimately, Tom joined the attorney's practice as a paralegal. Despite making less than he earned in the auto plant, Tom is happier than he's ever been. He's even thinking about taking courses that may lead someday to a law degree.

Take It Step by Step

A journey of a thousand miles begins with a single step.

Lao-Tsu
Dao De Jing

I T ' S   N O T   E A S Y to jump from one profession to another—nor to break into a career for the first time, particularly in bad economic times, when only the most credentialed people seem to have a chance of being hired. You may need to weave your new skills into your old profession. You need to build a staircase that will get you from here to there, step by step. The step-by-step approach is also critical if you're implementing a new business strategy within your organization or if you think you have a deficit in certain areas.

Anwar Hassan was a software engineer who always wanted to be a veterinarian. You may not know this, but statistically it's more difficult to become a practicing vet than it is to become a brain surgeon. But he was determined, and he succeeded by making one small move at a time. While continuing to work as a software engineer, Anwar volunteered at Angell Memorial, the premier animal hospital in the Boston area. He let people know about his computer skills, and gradually he built up a clientele of vets who needed help with their office and home computers. He applied to the University of Pennsylvania Veterinary School and got great references from these vets. Eventually, the combination of his degree, his computer skills, and the solid experience he'd gained working as a volunteer in the field paid off and he got the job of his dreams.

Remember, step by step. If you're a mechanic and you want to get into soap operas, there may be a way you can do it. But it's not likely to happen in a day. You've got to do it in nice digestible bites.

Take Your Show on the Road

But above all, try something.

Franklin Delano Roosevelt

A WONDERFUL WAY of finding out whether you'd really enjoy the job you're hankering to get is to take your show on the road. If you want a job that requires a lot of public speaking, give your first speech someplace other than your company's annual meeting. If you're going to propose to make your division a separate profit center, learn to read a balance sheet before you find yourself staring, bewildered, at your own.

Who will give you such valuable experience? There's a whole world of opportunities out there to learn valuable skills that may help you get a job—or figure out what kind of job you want. Volunteer to chair the fundraising auction at your daughter's school. Asking for donations will teach you a lot about sales. Writing fliers, catalogs, and thank-you notes will teach you about marketing communications. And figuring out payment procedures and balancing the books will give you a smattering of accounting skills.

Volunteer to serve on the finance committee for your church or temple. Offer to help a friend write a business plan for a new venture. Learn to give speeches without pain by joining a local Toastmasters Club. Offer to organize the entertainment at your class reunion. You can learn a lot in a much less threatening environment than your office—and you may find you can do some good as well.

Make a Job for Yourself

The business that we love we rise betime
And go to 't with delight.

William Shakespeare
Antony and Cleopatra

THE JOB YOU LOVE may be a job you create yourself. People who start their own businesses may often fail, but they rarely say they regret the experience. The perfect job for you may be a job you build by carefully analyzing your skills and passions, and by matching those to a need you see in the real world.

Bob Loomis worked in customer service at a paint and chemical manufacturing company, but his real passion was golf. He was determined to make a career out of golfing, but he wasn't a good enough golfer to play or teach the game professionally. He kept talking to people in the business, testing out different job ideas. Eventually, his list of contacts reached 75 or 80—people from golf ball companies, retailers, country clubs, pros on the tour, sportscasters, retired players, tournament organizers. He even wrote to Dinah Shore, a long-time entertainer, golfer, and organizer of celebrity tournaments, and she answered with some very nice suggestions for additional people he could talk to.

An idea, backed up by a strong dose of reality testing, finally emerged from Bob's efforts. He decided to try to build a business of golf industry customer service, blending his past experience with his passion for golf. He'd discovered that there was a great deal of work to be done whenever a golf tour or tournament came to town—establishing good relations with local hotels, restaurants, taxi and van companies, working with the local country clubs and golf courses, helping to make arrangements with local charities and civic organizations, serving as liaison to the local newspapers, working with local fundraisers, and more. The arrangements were usually made by a myriad of people, some more qualified than others, often with overlapping responsibilities. There was no consistent set of procedures or personnel from one town or tournament to the next. There was a need and he filled it. And the contacts he made during his career investigation also turned out to be extremely valuable once he established his new business.

An Exercise in Testing
a New Business Idea

1. If you're thinking about a new career, ask people who have that career what their day-to-day lives are like. Ask these people what they're doing now, what they did before, and what they expect to do next.

2. Where else can you find out more about your career goal? There are books, trade association journals, and directories; many good, general-purpose directories are listed in the last section of this book.

3. Where can you look for real answers to specific questions? If you're thinking of opening a gift store, for example, you'll want to ask such basic questions as:

   What is the inventory cost?

   What is the typical profit margin?

   What location is best?

   Do I need any additional training?

   Is there a big enough market for this shop in my area?

   Think critically about the answers to your questions.

4. Define your goal, and your plans for achieving your goal, as clearly as you can. If you define a plan in detail, it will suddenly look a lot more manageable.

5. Define an interim plan to keep you going while you go after a bigger objective. For example, if you've decided to get a law degree at night, try to carve out responsibilities in your current job that will increase your ability to be a good lawyer when the time comes. Perhaps you can try to work with your corporation's lawyers on a project, read contracts for your division, negotiate with suppliers, and write more memos.

6. Define a rough backup plan. What if your loan doesn't come through and you won't be able to start law school or your own business this year?

7. Explore the career or project you're interested in by actually doing it on a volunteer basis or part-time. Produce the fundraising literature for your college class, or write a column on a new technical area for your company newsletter. Figure out some way to do the job you may love while you continue in the job that pays the bills.

Tell Me a Story

*Draw your chair up close to the edge of the precipice
and I'll tell you a story.*

F. Scott Fitzgerald
Note-Books

WHAT MAKES YOU SPECIAL? Beyond your specific training, skills, and experience is a person and a set of personal qualities that make you what you are. These qualities, as much as the specifics of your work experience, determine what type of career and job will most satisfy and fulfill you. So, when you're searching for that job, don't hide those personal qualities. You owe it to yourself and to your prospective employer to let them shine through. They will illuminate the greyest credentials.

Many of the questions you'll be asked during your job hunt are predictable. Of course, you'll need to be prepared so you can answer these questions. But be sure to leave time to flesh out the dry recitation of facts and figures in your resumé and interviews to show the person behind the credentials.

In addition to telling what you've done in past jobs and other life experiences, show your potential employer *how* and *why* you did them:

> How did you make your job different?
> Why did you care about it?
> What creativity did you express in that job?
> How did it make you feel?
> How did you put your mark on that job?

Long after prospective employers have forgotten your resumé and the questions they have asked in an interview, they'll remember your story.

I worked once with a woman who had good credentials but was concerned that her heavy Romanian accent would deter interviewers. I asked her why she left her native country. It turned out that she had escaped under the most dangerous circumstances, and had emigrated to the United States, unable to speak any English at all. "I left Romania," she said, "because in that country working hard didn't help you get ahead. I wanted to live in a place where my hard work would let me amount to something." What a wonderful story, and what a wonderful personal touch to add to the mix of skills and experience she brought to her job hunt.

Need some help presenting a colorful and confident story of your own? Maybe this college application essay will inspire you. Hugh Gallagher wrote it as a student at Radnor High School in Newtown Square, PA. He went on to NYU, and his essay won first prize in the humor category of the 1990 Scholastic Writing Awards.

132

3A. ESSAY

IN ORDER FOR THE ADMISSIONS STAFF OF OUR COLLEGE TO GET TO KNOW YOU, THE APPLICANT, BETTER, WE ASK THAT YOU ANSWER THE FOLLOWING QUESTION: ARE THERE ANY SIGNIFICANT EXPERIENCES YOU HAVE HAD, OR ACCOMPLISHMENTS YOU HAVE REALIZED, THAT HAVE HELPED TO DEFINE YOU AS A PERSON?

I am a dynamic figure, often seen scaling walls and crushing ice. I have been known to remodel train stations on my lunch breaks, making them more efficient in the area of heat-retention. I translate ethnic slurs for Cuban refugees, I write award-winning operas, I manage time efficiently. Occasionally, I tread water for three days in a row.

I woo women with my sensuous and godlike trombone playing, I can pilot bicycles up severe inclines with unflagging speed, and I cook Thirty-Minute Brownies in twenty minutes. I am an expert in stucco, a veteran in love, and an outlaw in Peru.

Using only a hoe and a large glass of water, I once single-handedly defended a small village in the Amazon Basin from a horde of ferocious army ants. I play bluegrass cello, I was scouted by the Mets, I am the subject of numerous documentaries. When I'm bored, I build large suspension bridges in my yard. I enjoy urban hang gliding. On Wednesdays, after school, I repair electrical appliances free of charge.

I am an abstract artist, a concrete analyst, and a ruthless bookie. Critics worldwide swoon over my original line of corduroy evening wear. I don't perspire. I am a private citizen, yet I receive fan mail. I have been caller number nine and have won the weekend passes. Last summer I toured New Jersey with a traveling centrifugal-force demonstration. I bat .400. My deft floral arrangements have earned me fame in international botany circles. Children trust me.

I can hurl tennis rackets at small moving objects with deadly accuracy. I once read *Paradise Lost*, *Moby Dick*, and *David Copperfield* in one day and still had time to refurbish an entire dining room that evening. I know the exact location of every food item in the supermarket. I have performed several covert operations for the CIA. I sleep once a week; when I do sleep, I sleep in a chair. While on vacation in Canada, I successfully negotiated with a group of terrorists who had seized a small bakery. The laws of physics do not apply to me.

I balance, I weave, I dodge, I frolic, and my bills are all paid. On weekends, to let off steam, I participate in full-contact origami. Years ago I discovered the meaning of life but forgot to write it down. I have made extraordinary four-course meals using only a Mouli and a toaster oven. I breed prize winning clams. I have won bullfights in San Juan, cliff-diving competitions in Sri Lanka, and spelling bees at the Kremlin. I have played Hamlet, I have performed open-heart surgery, and I have spoken with Elvis.

But I have not yet gone to college.

Don't Try to Predict the Future

Trust no Future, howe'er pleasant!

Henry Wadsworth Longfellow
Resignation

WHAT IF YOU'RE LOOKING for your first job? What's a hot field right now? What should you learn? There's a traditional wisdom that says you should pick a career because there's a need for people in a particular field—computers, video repair, whatever. This scheme just doesn't work. Look at what happened in the 1950's and 60's. When Sputnik went up, America panicked. We set the kids to working on math and science, established scholarships, and sponsored special programs that would churn out the workers who would be needed by the next generation. Came the 70's and there was a glut of engineers, many of them wiped out by defense cuts and recessionary times. Then we turned them into teachers. The birth dearth took care of them, and now the teachers are turning to computer programming.

It's too hard to predict where the jobs are going to be—even a few years from now, once you've got your training. Of course you should pay attention to major trends. It's not too likely that illuminated manuscripts will make a major comeback. Computers are certainly here to stay. There will always be a need for doctors, cooks, and auto mechanics.

Sometimes, training for a career that's supposed to be hot right now is a way to avoid figuring out what you really want to do and what you're really best at doing. Do what most engages your attention—play your strong suit. Even in a bad economy, remember that there's always room for special people in every profession. If you're really good at what you do, and if you keep learning to be even better, the world will know about it.

Who Do You Know?

"NETWORKING" IS a new name for an old game. It means talking, calling, meeting, contacting, asking, listening, schmoozing—it's the personal side of career and job hunting. An awesome 70 percent of all jobs are filled through personal contacts, and I'll bet 90 percent or more of the jobs people really love are found this way.

Many job hunters think that networking is for CEOs, venture capitalists, and movie stars—not for humble secretaries, graphic designers, and day care workers. They don't think they *have* any worthwhile contacts. "I don't have any network," they say. "I don't belong to professional organizations. I don't go to conferences. I'm not a member of the Elks."

Wrong! Everybody has networks. Everybody is a member of many constituencies. You have relatives. You live in a neighborhood. I'll bet some of your relatives and neighbors know people who work, or have friends who work, in industries you'd like to know more about. Do you go to church or temple? A gym? Do you have a hairdresser, a lawyer, a plumber? Maybe they have friends. Did you ever have a job? Where are your coworkers now? Don't assume that only people who work in your own field can help in your job search. Everybody has a web of connections. Through one path or another, you may find the connection of most value to you.

A Networking Inventory:
Who Do You Know?

Business Contacts:

- Coworkers—remember, there may be confidentiality issues
- Former coworkers—bosses, peers, subordinates
- Business acquaintances, even competitors
- Business vendors (company lawyer, accountant, insurance agent, suppliers)
- Business clients and customers

Personal Contacts:

- Relatives
- Personal friends
- Personal business consultants (lawyer, accountant, insurance agent, banker, real estate broker)
- Personal service consultants (doctor, dentist, psychiatrist, hairdresser, barber, veterinarian)
- Home and car maintenance consultants (plumber, mechanic, carpenter, gardener)
- Athletic contacts (people at your gym, on your teams)
- Friends and business contacts of your spouse
- Teachers of your children
- Parents of your children's friends, classmates, and teammates
- Your minister, priest, or rabbi, and people in the congregation
- Former classmates in high school, college, and graduate school
- Former classmates at any training sessions or seminars you've attended
- Faculty and administrators you knew at any schools you've attended
- Social acquaintances
- Neighbors
- Friends and neighbors of your parents and other relatives
- Anybody else on your holiday card list

Membership Contacts (members of any of these groups):

- Professional organizations (American Chemical Society, computer society, writing group, etc.)
- Political organizations (town meeting, local campaign groups, etc.)
- Social welfare or public affairs organizations (local environmental club, etc.)

- Cultural organizations (drama, orchestra, ballet, opera, etc.)
- Community organizations (Elks, Scouts, etc.)
- Veterans organizations (VFW, etc.)
- Hobby organizations (ham radio, stamp club, etc.)
- School organizations (e.g., fraternities, sororities, teams, volunteer groups, etc.)

Community/College Contacts:

- Local politicians (in your own community or the community you'd like to work in)
- Local merchants, especially the local newspaper people
- Local Chamber of Commerce or other business organizations
- College alumni/ae association
- Staff of your college career planning office

Add your own categories:

_____

_____

_____

_____

_____

_____

_____

_____

_____

_____

Make That Connection

I, Sir, am a person of most respectable connections.

Samuel Butler
A Psalm of Montreal

THERE IS AN ADAGE that says that everybody is only two phone calls away from everybody else. The idea is that somebody knows somebody who knows somebody.

You never know who'll help the most. A few years ago, I worked with a client, Janet Madrosian, whose specialty was clean room manufacturing. ("Clean rooms" are those in which air is filtered, and technicians wear masks and special suits designed to keep dust from affecting the manufacturing of electronic or other sensitive components.) Janet was working at the time for a computer manufacturer whose business was in decline. I had been counseling her about exploring new industries and building her networking skills. One afternoon, she took time out for the hairdresser. Janet commented there that she was so stressed out these days that having her hair done was an especially welcome treat. She ended up chatting with Stella, the hairdresser, about her job search, and Stella introduced her to Rita Winston, who was waiting in the next chair. "Rita does something high-tech too," said Stella. This isn't a complete Cinderella story. Rita's company, a manufacturer of industrial laser technology, didn't actually hire Janet. But Rita did give Janet several suggestions for contacts, and one of them, who worked for the laser company's optical supplier, eventually hired Janet to work in the clean room manufacturing of telescope lenses—a less volatile industry than computers, and one Janet enjoyed greatly.

At every seminar and workshop I teach, at least one or two people in the audience share their own stories about serendipitous connections. At one recent workshop, a participant recounted the story of how he had looked unsuccessfully for a night bartending job to supplement the income from his day paralegal job. One day, riding in the elevator in his law firm's building, he ran into an old high school classmate. They chatted, and the paralegal mentioned his search for a job. "My wife's brother owns the bar at the Radisson next door," said his old classmate. "Want to take a walk over there? I think he's looking for somebody." Sure enough, within an hour, the paralegal-by-day was a bartender-by-night.

An Exercise in Networking

Your most promising route to a job you love is through the power of networking. Once you've put together a list of contacts, what do you say to them? Every networking conversation is different, but here are some basic guidelines:

Tell them (briefly):

1. Why you're contacting them.
2. About your background.
3. About the career/job you hope to find.
4. About where you've applied, and what resources you've used (e.g., agencies) so far.

Ask them:

1. Would you be willing to give me names of people who might be able to advise me about my job search? Ask if you can use your contact's name; then, when you call, you can say "So-and-so suggested that I call you because . . ." (If you feel comfortable doing so, you might also ask if your contact will call ahead to introduce you.)
2. Would you give me names of people in your organization, or in organizations you're familiar with, so I can send them resumés? Again, ask if you can use your contact's name and, perhaps, if your contact will introduce you.
3. Do you know of any meetings I could attend?
4. If you were me, who else would you talk to?
5. Where would you look for published openings (newspapers, magazines, libraries, databases, inhouse bulletin boards, etc.)?
6. If your contact works at a company you're interested in pursuing: Does your own company have an inhouse bulletin board of job postings? Would you be willing to check that board for me?
7. Are there any employment agencies you'd recommend? Any you'd avoid?

Leave them:

1. A copy of your resumé (so they'll know how to get in touch with you or be able to pass it on, if appropriate).
2. Your thanks—and don't forget to follow up with a thank you note—now and again when you do get the job.
3. A promise that you will return the favor in the future.

Who Gets Hired?

And what are his qualifications— ONE
He's the Earl of Fitzdotterel's eldest son.

Robert Barnabas Brough
My Lord Tomnoddy

WHO GETS HIRED? The most qualified person—yes or no? Quite often, no. When a nuclear power plant is hiring a technician, do they need a nuclear physicist? Of course not. What they want is someone whose skills are sufficient. Someone who can clear the bar. Someone whose mix of education, training, work experience, personal characteristics, personal history, and outside interests fits the job.

Sometimes, years of experience can almost be a handicap. I ran into this when I visited the former Soviet Union in the summer of 1991. The service was unexpectedly superb at a hotel in Saint Petersburg that was being funded through a Swedish joint venture. I asked the manager how he found his people. "I hire people with no experience at all," he told me. "I look for people who are cheerful and upbeat, people who like dealing with other people. I don't want anyone who's worked in a hotel before. They have too many bad habits."

Paper qualifications are often less important than personal qualities. You need the minimum requirements, that's true. But you're being hired into an existing group, and that group is looking for more than just technical skills. They want you to fit in. They're going to be looking not just for the person with the most years on the job, but for the person with the personal qualities—intelligence, hard work, a sense of humor, an ability to grow in a job—that will create the best fit with existing people and projects in the organization.

Once the basic credentials are there, they'll be hiring *the person*. You can be that person.

Hunting for a job isn't brain surgery. People just like you—and people without half your gifts—hunt successfully for jobs every day. So can you. And the more you work at it, the better you'll get at it. Even in a bad economy, you will succeed at finding a job you love if you identify clearly what's right for your own mix of skills and personality, and you work hard at finding the right job match.

Go Outside for Help

Advice is seldom welcome; and those who [need]
it the most always like it the least.

Philip Dormer Stanhope, Earl of Chesterfield
Letters

IF YOU'VE EVER WATCHED someone drive around the same block four times in a row looking for an address, you'll understand why so many people end up stuck in jobs they don't like. Sometimes, it's emotionally easier to pretend you know where you're going than it is to stop and ask for help figuring things out. If you do decide that you need help—more than that of friends and coworkers—to get you going on a new path, you'll find lots of professional resources out there.

But, before you spend one penny on professional help, see what you can get for free. Your college probably has an alumni association or a career placement center that offers counseling, workshops, discussion groups, and possibly job referrals and mentoring programs. You may qualify even if you've been out of school for many years. Professional organizations may sponsor evening or breakfast meetings to allow their members to network for jobs, advice, and support. Groups like Jewish Vocational Services (you don't need to be Jewish to use them), the Women's Educational and Industrial Union (you don't need to be a woman), and others offer free or low-cost career groups and counseling. There are women's groups, men's groups, parents' groups, church groups, minority groups, social organization groups, and all manner of self-help groups—many of them completely free. There are special groups for people who have been fired, people who are returning to the job market after an absence, and people who fear they're too old to find jobs. Your employer may even offer career development groups.

Push yourself to give these groups a try. If you're lucky, you'll find professional networking contacts as well as moral support. Among people who find themselves in the same boat as you, you may be able to express some of the anger, fear, and frustration that you're feeling in your job or your job search. You may also find that having to report back to a group each week will spur you to work harder that week. This is the philosophy behind Weight Watchers and many other kinds of self-help groups. If nothing else, such groups may give you a welcome feeling that you're not alone.

Be a Wise and Wary Consumer of Professional Help

Good counsellors lack no clients.

William Shakespeare
Measure for Measure

IT'S FUNNY HOW we talk to more people about where to bring our cars to be fixed than we do about where to bring ourselves.

You may eventually decide that you need the services of a paid vocational counselor. These people can administer formal aptitude tests, skills assessments, and career selection profiles, which you may find very useful if you're not sure what career path to follow. Some of the tests you may hear about are the Myers-Briggs Type Indicator, the Career Assessment Inventory (CAI) 16 PF (Personality Factor), the Strong-Campbell Vocational Interest Blank (SCVIB), and the AVL Study of Values. You should be aware that counselors are often very expensive and that the vocational testing and advisory profession is totally unregulated. You'll need to be a wise consumer if you use vocational services. Be sure to talk to other people who have used these services. Make certain that the people you consult have been satisfied with the counseling they've received.

If you've been laid off, you may be entitled to professional outplacement counseling services. Outplacement has become a billion dollar business. There are hundreds of firms offering outplacement services, ranging from job-hunting workshops and use of office space and secretarial services to hand holding for the manager who's laying off staff. If you're laid off or fired, ask if outplacement services are available to you. You may find them helpful.

An Exercise in Finding Professional Help

Consider asking these questions before you sign up for any professional vocational and counseling services:

1. Tell me about your firm. What exactly do you do? How long have you been in business?

2. How many people do you employ? What is their educational background? Their years in business? What associations do they belong to? What special awards or certifications have they received?

3. How many clients have you had? How many have had job histories and skills similar to mine?

4. What is the success rate for people like me?

5. What methods do you use (individual counseling, classes, specific tests, techniques, etc.)?

6. What exactly will I get for my money? Over what period?

7. What are your charges? What is the schedule of payment?

8. Are there any guarantees? What if I don't think you've helped me? Will I get my money back, or some portion of it? Will you give me any additional services?

9. Can you give me some references—for both the organization as a whole and the individual counselors? (Be sure to follow up on these references and find out how satisfied or dissatisfied they were with the firm.)

Don't Let Others' Judgments Hold You Back

*The only jobs for which no man is qualified are human incubator
and wet nurse. Likewise, the only job for which no woman is or
can be qualified is sperm donor.*

Wilma Scott Heide
NOW Official Biography

SO FEW THINGS are really beyond our grasp. Yet many people try to convince us that we can't do what we want to do. When somebody says you don't have the right experience, education, personality, or background, try to assess whether there might be biases, prejudices, and unfair stereotypes underlying the message.

Despite the talk about diversity and affirmative action in this country, most corporate jobs are still white, male, and ethnocentric. Only a few years ago, an executive search consultant I knew refused to even present a highly qualified candidate to his corporate client. The reason? The candidate was of Italian descent and the consultant told me, "He wouldn't fit into the corporate culture." The sad thing is, the consultant's perception was accurate: he would not have been welcome in the overwhelmingly WASPy environment.

Our educational establishments are confronting the future a lot more clearly and directly than is industry. More and more schools—from elementary and high schools to community colleges to medical and law schools—are enrolling more and more women, people of color, foreign students, gay and lesbian students, and those with physical handicaps. Schools have been forced, in many cases by federal funding statutes, to expand the boundaries of education.

Except for the armed forces, "adult" organizations have been slower to move in the direction of diversity. Women and minorities are slowly making their ways up the corporate ladder, but most report that the "glass ceiling" at the top of that ladder is thicker than ever. There are some exceptions, particularly in forward-looking professions like high-tech. Sandra Kurtzig of Ask and Carol Bartz of Autodesk are two examples of women who have broken into the CEO ranks. But such success stories are still few and far between.

When Golda Meir was asked by the Knesset whether she thought she could do as good a job as a man, as Prime Minister of Israel, she replied, "I certainly couldn't do any worse." That wonderful self-confidence helped her surmount many obstacles—and win many hearts—during her successful career.

Laid Off or Set Free?

When I lost my job, I was numb for about an hour. I felt nothing at all. Then, little by little, feeling returned. And I've got to admit, what I felt first was just plain relief.

Paul Thompson, laid off from a manufacturing plant

YOU MIGHT EXPECT the emotions felt by people who have been fired or laid off to be disappointment, anger, and fear. And of course these feelings do dominate. But, of the many thousands of "outplaced" people I've counseled, I would say more than half of them have another reaction as well. Despite their natural anxiety about the job market and whether they'll be able to find new jobs, these people often feel a strong sense of relief. They've disliked their jobs so intensely that, at the most fundamental level, they're just happy they won't have to work at these jobs any more. Here's what they have to say:

I couldn't make the move on my own, but I'm relieved that I'm finally being forced to find a job I like better. (A secretary in an ad agency)

I hated the place. I don't know why I stayed so long. (An engineer who worked for the government)

I'm glad it's over. (A marketing manager for a high-tech company

What a relief not to have to work with those jerks any more. (A mechanic at an auto repair shop)

Free at last! (A public high school Spanish teacher)

If you've lost your job, let your feelings work for you. Resolve that your next job will be a job you love, not a job you'd be relieved to lose.

Is There Life Outside Your Job?

There *is* life outside of work. Loving a job doesn't mean you need to give all your time and all your energy to that job. The best jobs expand your energy, rather than sapping it. They make you a happier person—a person who wants to share that happiness with family and friends, and who wants to extend out into the community and the larger world.

But jobs you love can often be exhausting. To keep your own job in balance, you need to keep your eye on all the balls you juggle in your life. And you need to take a little time out for yourself—to recharge your batteries and have some fun.

Become a Juggler

The world is so full of a number of things,
I'm sure we should all be as happy as kings.

Robert Louis Stevenson
A Child's Garden of Verses

SOME PEOPLE TALK about leading a balanced life. I prefer to think of it as a juggling act, with four very different balls in the air:

1. Your work life—your day-to-day work and your long-term striving for a career that satisfies you.

2. Your home life—the emotional needs of your family members, as well as all the logistics of cleaning, laundry, carpooling, pet care, lawnmowing, and so on and on and on.

3. Your social life—your friends, your volunteer activities, and your extension into various communities (town, neighborhood, schools, organizations, etc.)

4. Your individual life—your intellectual and spiritual feelings, values, goals, and dreams. At the deepest level, who are you? Do you like who you are? Where are you going?

A convenient way of viewing the world in which you juggle your work, home, social, and individual balls is what I call your "lifespace" (see the diagram on the next page).

Sometimes you've got your hand on one ball, sometimes another. Some days or weeks or even years, one part of your life predominates. If you're doing a medical internship and are on call every other night, you're not likely to be spending much quality time learning a new language or volunteering at a local shelter; you may have trouble remembering your children's names and brushing your teeth! The same is true if you're running a small business or opening a new office or starting a new job in a fast-growing company.

In the months after the birth of a new baby, you may be in a very different mode. Whether you're male or female, back at work or staying home, your primary focus is very likely to be that new life that needs nurturing and demands not only your time but also your single-minded emotional energy.

During other phases of your life, you may be able to maintain a more balanced load, trading off working, childraising, spending time with your family and friends, cleaning house, learning something new, helping somebody who needs a lift, and otherwise filling your life with time-consuming activities, sometimes frustrating, sometimes euphoric, but always demanding.

The Lifespace

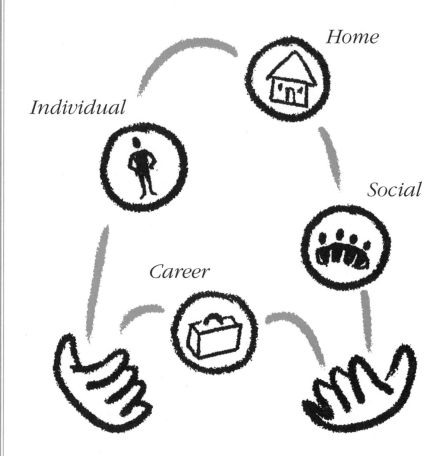

Home

Individual

Social

Career

For each of the balls you're juggling, you'll need to:

- Clarify your own values regarding work, home, etc.
- Set the goals you want to achieve in all the areas you value.
- Figure out which abilities you already have, and which you need to develop, to achieve your goals.
- Assess whether any of your own personal needs are still unmet after all your juggling.

Juggling Can Be Good for You

Too many people, too many demands, too much to do.

Anne Morrow Lindbergh
Bring Me a Unicorn

THE NOTION OF WORKING people as jugglers is an especially apt metaphor for working mothers.

In *Juggling,* Faye J. Crosby looks at the world of women who juggle work and home life. With increasing opportunities for women in the business world and new patterns of home and child care come new challenges to coordinate the often conflicting demands on women's time and energy. Crosby looks at volumes of research and finds that, despite the stresses of lack of time and support, women—and their children—actually benefit from their multiple roles. She says:

> *Combining paid employment with marriage and motherhood creates safeguards for emotional well-being. Nothing is certain in life, but generally the chances of happiness are greater if one has multiple areas of interest and involvement. To juggle is to diminish the risk of depression, anxiety, and unhappiness.*

In addition to making life more interesting, juggling the balls of work and home life seems to make working women feel more capable and sure of themselves. Competence in one area carries over to the other. And, on the other hand, a setback in one area may be compensated for by a success in the other.

What's the catch? To enjoy your multiple roles, you need support from both your job and home. And too few working people—women or men—receive it. In one study by Priority Management, a Seattle-based consulting firm, 85 percent of middle managers polled reported that they found it hard to lead balanced lives, with time for work, home, society, and themselves. Only one in 50 said they were now successfully juggling everything!

Live the Only Life You've Got

I could not at any age be content to take my place in a corner by the fireside and simply look on. Life was meant to be lived. One must never, for whatever reason, turn one's back on life.

Eleanor Roosevelt

ELEANOR ROOSEVELT lived a lonely childhood and a difficult married life, with a domineering mother-in-law and a disabled and unfaithful husband. Yet, despite personal hardships, she lived her life to the fullest, giving back to her country a legacy of productivity and zest that no other First Lady has yet equalled.

Mrs. Roosevelt never accepted her lot in life—either professional or personal. During FDR's career, she gave her own life meaning by working actively on issues of great importance to her. She was always more than just the First Lady, an appendage to her successful husband. Long after her husband's death, and the end of her official obligations, she played a continuing role in national and international affairs. She believed firmly, with Oliver Wendell Holmes, Jr., that all people must "share the passion and action of (their) time at peril of being judged not to have lived." When Mrs. Roosevelt died, Adlai Stevenson said about her:

> *She would rather light a candle than curse the darkness, and her glow has warmed the world.*

You may encounter setbacks—in your career and in your personal life. You may be tempted to turn back from the challenges presented by these setbacks, to sit by the fireside and wait them out. Or you may choose to confront these challenges directly: to face them with grace, energy, and humor.

Life Isn't Always Fair

*Everything has two handles—one by which it may be
borne; another by which it cannot.*

Epictetus
The Encheiridion

WHEN YOU'RE YOUNG and just starting out in a profession, you may find it easy to dream big, to work with single-minded concentration, and to think positively about overcoming all odds—at work and throughout your life. But what happens when you encounter obstacles, when you get sick, when your children get in trouble, when life seems to be too much for you? How do you keep working when your personal life is in ruins?

I point to Stephen Hawking when people ask, "How can I work under these circumstances?" Hawking has earned an international reputation as the most brilliant theoretical physicist since Einstein, and is known to many millions of readers around the world as the author of the best-selling *A Brief History of Time*. And he has accomplished these feats while suffering his whole adult life from the degenerative disease, amyotrophic lateral sclerosis (ALS), named "Lou Gehrig's disease" after it struck baseball great Lou Gehrig.

The onslaught of Hawking's disease would have overwhelmed most people, both physically and mentally. But during the years of physical deterioration, Hawking has made great strides towards finding the "Theory of Everything," a theory that has been the quest of theoretical physicists since Einstein's time. Through his writings, he has also made physics concepts accessible to millions of non-scientists. Far from railing at the unfairness of his illness, or using it as an excuse for poor professional performance, Hawking simply moved on to make the best of his situation. One of Hawking's many biographers, Kitty Ferguson, recounts Hawking's words: "One has to be grown up enough to realize that life is not fair. You just have to do the best you can in the situation you are in."

Once he had come to terms with his illness and realized that he could live many years with it, Hawking actually found that he could move on and live life to the fullest: "I suddenly realized that there were a lot of worthwhile things I could do, if I were reprieved . . . although there was a cloud hanging over my future, I found to my surprise that I was enjoying life in the present more than before." Hawking even credits his physical deterioration with helping him to focus his mind and concentrate on physics theory in a way that he claims would be more difficult if he were expected to carry on ordinary day-to-day activities.

Hawking's amazing story reminds me of what Robert Louis Stevenson said:

*Even if the doctor does not give you a year, even if he hesitates about a
month, make one brave push and see what can be accomplished in a week.*

Play the Hand That's
Dealt You

Life is not the way it's supposed to be. It's the way it is.
The way you cope with it is what makes the difference.

Virginia Satir

IN A PERFECT WORLD, our jobs would always be lucrative and personally rewarding. Our bosses would never be short-tempered or ignorant. Our colleagues would never be jealous or mean-spirited. Our subordinates would never be shirkers or malingerers. But we don't live in a perfect world, and on some days in some jobs, this is painfully apparent.

This isn't the way it should be, we complain. Unfortunately, though, every day and every job has its unpleasant realities. There are aspects to our jobs, our bosses, our colleagues, and our subordinates, that we just can't change and we have to endure. If, on balance, these annoyances make us dislike our jobs, it's time to make a move. But if we love our jobs, most days in most ways, then we've got to find a way to handle the ups and downs.

Sometimes the ups and downs of life are very serious ones, at work and in our lives. The way we handle these vicissitudes will make or break us. One of our most basic expectations is that we come into this world with parents. But, it doesn't always work that way. Two very different world leaders lost their fathers before they were born: Bill Clinton and Sadam Hussein. Surely there were many other influences—familial and cultural—on these two, but it is interesting to note the parallel. Both rose to fame in their own countries. But President Clinton perhaps learned from the experience that life is uncertain—and that we must therefore protect and nurture it. Sadam Hussein appears to have learned the opposite lesson—that the uncertainty of life cheapens it.

Don't Live Somebody Else's Dream

Be so true to thyself as thou be not false to others.

Francis Bacon
Of Wisdom for a Man's Self

SOMETIMES, instead of making our own dreams come true, we find ourselves living out the dreams of our family—or other people we care about.

The Vartanian family has been in the auto leasing company since Grandfather V arrived in this country as a penniless immigrant and built a small equipment lending business into a successful and varied leasing business. Armen, the son, went happily into the business and developed it still more. Ed, the grandson, worked towards a business degree in the expectation of taking over the business himself someday. But after Ed worked in the leasing company for a few years, he began to question the assumption that he'd spend the rest of his life walking in his father's and grandfather's footsteps.

Ed finally decided that he couldn't be happy in the business and started thinking about what he really wanted to do. He felt a lot of responsibility to the family, though, and he also thought carefully about what would happen to the business without him. He discussed his dilemma with other people in the family. One young cousin, Sara, who was attending business school, told him that she'd always wanted to run a business of her own. Bingo! Ed decided to stay in the business until his cousin had her degree and had been able to prove that she'd eventually be capable of taking over the business. He also decided to go part-time to the Museum of Fine Arts School to pursue a life-long interest in drawing.

Several years have passed, Sara is doing very well learning the ropes, and, interestingly enough, Ed is still in the business and happy about it, now that he doesn't feel the full weight of responsibility on his shoulders. He was able to let go of the pressures upon him enough to think about what he really wanted to do in his life. For now, he's working and going to school. He thinks he might eventually combine his business skill and his artistic interest into gallery ownership or some other blended career. Now that he no longer feels responsible for the ultimate fate of the business, he's able to take the time to think about where his dreams will lead him.

Time to Move On

It is a mark of many famous people that they cannot part with their brightest hour: what worked once must always work.

Lillian Hellman
Pentimento

LEARN FROM YOUR PAST, but don't dwell on past experiences. Both the triumphs and the tragedies in our past lives can hold us back. Many of us have failed to get the full measure of love, success, and satisfaction that we wanted in our lives. We can dwell on those disappointments, or we can move on. Before you can triumph—in your job or your life—you've got to forgive yourself and the people who have disappointed you—parents, teachers, old friends, old bosses. You've got to make a conscious decision to let it go.

We may need to let go of the success stories and the dreams of our youths as well. How many of us have made our livings doing what our high school yearbooks predicted for us? The "most likely to succeed" didn't. We got fat and we ended up working for somebody else. Are we losers? Of course not. Remember your "glory days" with pleasure, and relive them from time to time. But don't feel, like the jocks in Bruce Springsteen's song, that it's all downhill from there. You're not living out the fantasy of your childhood and teenage years; you're living the life of an adult. You can still dream and aspire to be what your adult self wants to be.

Sometimes it's very difficult to put childhood issues behind us and to go on to live happy and productive adult lives. Try your best to put the past behind you and start again. If you can't get rid of the baggage of your past history, even with the help of family and friends, you might want to consider talking it out with a professional counselor or a therapist. Otherwise, you may find your future goals crippled by your past experiences.

An Exercise in Letting Go

1. Complete the following sentences:

    "If only I had . . ."

    "My biggest drawback has always been . . ."

    "What's holding me back is . . ."

    Here are some sentences from people I've counseled:

    "If only I had an MBA."

    "If only I had my sister's personality."

    "My biggest drawback is that I'm shy."

    "My biggest drawback is that I'm deaf."

    "My biggest drawback is that I didn't finish college."

    "What's holding me back is my boss."

    "What's holding me back are my family commitments."

2. Review your own answers. Are any of your answers "decoys" for your true feelings? Does your sister really have a more winning personality, or do you resent her for having had an easier childhood? Is your boss really holding you back, or are you frightened about looking for another job?

3. Can you do anything about your regrets? If you *can* do something, do it! Put together an action plan. If you need more education, you *can* find a way. It may take years to get your degree part-time, but it can be done. If you're shy or lack confidence, try speaking out with your friends. Take a seminar or course that will force you to make presentations. In some cases, counseling may help you overcome, or at least help you understand, some of the traits you dislike in yourself.

4. Maybe you *can't* change your situation: your physical handicaps, your family, the time you got going on your career track. But maybe you can come to better terms with your history or about the pressures or regrets you feel.

    And maybe there just isn't anything to be done. You aren't your sister and you never will be. Admit that your feelings about your past are unnecessary baggage. As with any other journey, your journey through life doesn't need this baggage. If you can't change things, let these feelings go!

Just Say No

Qu'est-ce qu'un homme révolté? Un homme qui dit non.
What is a rebel? A man who says no.

Albert Camus
The Rebel

EVERYBODY LIKES TO SAY YES. As e.e. cummings put it, "yes is a pleasant country." Throughout this book, we've encouraged you to say yes—yes to opening your mind and dreaming about a new career and larger goals, yes to learning new skills, yes to helping other people find a better life for themselves.

But sometimes you've got to say no. At some point, you need to set limits—not on your own aspirations, but on the demands other people place upon you. There's only so much you can do each day, each week, each year, and in your lifetime. Everyone has expectations of you—some reasonable and some not so reasonable. You've got to separate one from the other. You can't squander all your precious time fulfilling other peoples' dreams—if those dreams are not also your own. Remember that old saying, "You can please all of the people some of the time, and some of the people all of the time, but you can't please all of the people all of the time." You can accomplish a tremendous amount. But *you* must be the one to decide what to do and how much to do. Make sure you're not working so hard at pleasing other people that you never please yourself.

I had the pleasure several years ago of meeting the grande dame of cookery, Julia Child. She told me that she was under constant pressure to do more. People were always asking her to expand her repertoire by doing books and television presentations on cuisines other than that of France. She said she had refused all such offers. "I can only do so much," she told me. "I've got to set limits in order to do something—one thing—really well." So she sticks very sensibly and deliciously to French cooking, letting other people explore Mexico, Asia, pizza, and tofu.

Sometimes, the expectations placed upon us are, if not reasonable, par for the course, and you've got to figure out if that's the course you want to be on. Law firms are notorious for chewing up their young associates; 100-plus hours a week is often the going rate. Medical interns and residents routinely go without sleep every other night. There may not be a lot you can do about this wretched pattern and still get where you want to go. You've got to decide whether, at this particular point in your life, this is a sacrifice that you can stand, or one that will break you, your family, and your sense of self.

An Exercise in Saying No

Some expectations are unreasonable, and you need to learn to say no when the requests become unacceptable to you. Here are some examples:

1. Your boss—Some managers are unreasonable and seem to take a devilish pleasure in piling load upon load of work on the shoulders of their subordinates. Most are not. Some of us take every suggestion from our managers as a directive and then panic when we're not able to get everything done. Whenever your boss asks you to do anything, find out the priority of the work. If you're overloaded with high-priority items already, ask about rearranging the items in your list. You're not saying no to your new task—only to adding it right now to the top of an already toppling pile.

2. Your subordinates—Some people want more support than you can reasonably give them. They're always late. They always need help. They always ask the same questions. Managers who have an open-door policy may find that these employees are always wandering in, asking to talk about their assignments. Set legitimate limits on the amount of help and support you give your subordinates, and then enforce those limits.

3. Your peers—Everybody likes to be liked. Sometimes we're so eager to be liked by our coworkers that we're too quick to offer or agree to help. Let somebody else take a turn.

4. Community groups—Sometimes you just have to say no to adding one more obligation to your plate. Community service organizations want you to canvas for funds in your neighborhood; your local homeless shelter wants you to cook and serve one night a week; your child's school wants you to go on a field trip; the American Red Cross wants you to give a pint of blood; your college wants you to join its mentor program. You want to do it all—and it all needs to be done. But if you never say no, if you keep adding more and more obligations, the well will run dry. You've got to keep some time for yourself and your family.

Don't Burn Your Candle
at Both Ends

It takes all the running you can do to keep in the same place.
If you want to get somewhere else you must run twice
as fast as that.

Alice, in Lewis Carroll's
Through the Looking Glass

WITH THE EVER-INCREASING demands of your boss, your family, and your community, as well as your own demands on yourself, you may feel more and more like Alice.

I was once brought in to consult at a space-age composite materials company I'll call New Nylon Technologies (NNT). The company had developed a state-of-the-art technology at great cost and long hours from its small staff. It was clear that NNT could not bring the product to market by itself and that the company would have to be acquired by a larger company with extensive financial resources. All of the senior management team owned a piece of the company, as did many of the technicians. The tension of running the business while courting large companies and the venture capital community extracted a heavy toll.

My assignment was to work with Charles Kenyon, the vice-president of manufacturing, to help him moderate his increasingly frequent outbursts. His barking of orders to anyone within earshot was worthy of Captain Bligh. It happened that I was on site the day that a U.S. Navy officer was touring the facility, evaluating the company's product. We were talking about our military backgrounds when one of Charles' outbursts erupted in a nearby office. The Lieutenant Commander glanced at me and commented under his breath, "Boy, this guy must be due for a little R&R."

The U.S. military is not exactly the archetype of a warm and fuzzy organization. But even our Pentagon realizes that, no matter how skilled or motivated the military man or woman, there is a point at which rest and relaxation is mandatory. Without it, the well-being of an entire mission is at risk. Clearly, Charles had reached the point of needing emergency R&R.

Time Out

To burn always with this hard, gemlike flame,
to maintain this ecstasy, is success in life.

Walter Pater
Conclusion

YOU CAN'T ALWAYS BURN with a hard, gemlike flame.

Some people seem to have boundless energy, taking on more and more projects, all of which they perform with verve and intensity—like Percy in Shakespeare's *Henry IV, Part I,*

> *...the Hotspur of the North; he that kills me some six or seven dozen of Scots. At a breakfast, washes his hands, and says to his wife, "Fie upon this quiet life! I want work."*

When you love what you do, it's sometimes hard to stop and take a break. But, when we're always operating in high gear, piling on stress after stress without respite, we run the risk of burning out.

Many American business consultants tell us that U.S. workers and managers should be mimicking their Japanese counterparts, whose devotion to work and quality are becoming legendary. And yet, currently, top Japanese business and government leaders are trying to stem the growing tide of *karoshi*, the tendency of a growing number of Japanese "salarymen" to drop dead of overwork. The Japanese mass media are now pushing novel concepts of taking additional vacation time and spending more time with families.

Interestingly enough, U.S. and Japanese workers put in very close to the same number of hours per week (40 for the U.S., 41.5 for Japan) and take close to the same number of paid vacation days per year (12 for the U.S., 11 for Japan). By contrast, German workers put in an average of only 37.6 hours per week and take 30 paid vacation days per year. (Statistics from the Institute of the German Economy in Cologne).

Working Longer Doesn't Mean Working Better

Work expands so as to fill the time available for its completion.

C. Northcote Parkinson
Parkinson's Law

MOST OF US WORK many more hours than our parents did. As layoffs, downsizing, and international competition have become a more prominent part of the corporate landscape, the pressure to work harder—or at least longer—is great. In a *Fortune* poll of CEOs, 58 percent of respondents said they expected high-level executives in their organizations to work 50 to 59 hours per week; 29 percent expected 60 hours or more; 21 percent of these CEOs expected their middle managers to put in 41 to 49 hours per week; 53 percent expected 50 to 59 hours.

In *The Overworked American*, Juliet Schor points out that there is no evidence that increased hours leads to increased productivity. In fact, working longer may have the opposite effect; as you work longer, you lose concentration and may make poorer decisions—witness the recent movement to control the huge number of hours medical interns and residents put in on the job.

In American corporations, busyness seems to equal importance; 80 hours a week is the ultimate status symbol in some professions. I once worked for an organization where the boss would comment to people leaving at 6:00 p.m., "Only working a half day today?"

Keep Recharging Your Batteries

Rest, rest, perturbed spirit.

William Shakespeare
Hamlet

YOU MIGHT THINK that people who truly love their jobs want to spend all their time doing those jobs. Oddly enough, the people who love their jobs the most are people who make room in their lives for things other than work. Workaholics usually get little real enjoyment from what they do. Sometimes their work is an escape from other parts of their lives. Actually, workaholism is an overused term. A larger problem is overwork—trying to do too much, in too little time, with too little support, and too few resources.

The people who really love their jobs—and who *keep* loving those jobs over time—are the people who can manage their time, get help when they need it, and save some time for themselves. We all need to keep recharging our physical, mental, and emotional batteries. If you burn out early, you'll be of little value to your organization, to those close to you, and to yourself.

In Greek mythology, the gods designed a cruel way to punish Sisyphus. He was condemned to spend his lifetime pushing a heavy boulder to a mountaintop, only to have it roll down to the bottom where he'd have to begin again, and again, and again. Evidently, even the pantheon of ancient Greek gods could think of no more painful punishment than to be engaged perpetually in fruitless, hopeless, and futile work. Yet many of us believe that it is just this behavior that will bring us success in our work lives.

Stella Johnson was an intelligent and resourceful high-school graduate who started her career as a secretary at a respected monthly magazine. She later became a fact checker and, eventually, director of research. Stella took her work so seriously that she couldn't find time for anything else: personal relationships, entertainment, exercise. She couldn't say no to any assignment, and she couldn't seem to trust her subordinates to carry through on important projects. She was self-conscious about her education—though, realistically, her lack of a degree wasn't a drawback to her work. As the years went by, Stella worked longer and longer hours and never could find the time to take a vacation. Her only relief was in eating, and she ballooned to more than 200 pounds. Stella was clearly on the road to burnout.

Research shows that the people who suffer the most from burnout are the most committed and responsible employees, those who don't pass the buck. Burnout is seen frequently in the helping professions—doctors, nurses, hospital workers, social workers, teachers.

An Exercise: Are You Suffering Burnout?

How can you recognize burnout? Ask yourself these questions:

1. Do you often feel hopeless?
2. Do you often feel confused or conflicted about where you're going?
3. Do you often feel physically exhausted during the work day or at the end of the day?
4. Do you often feel disillusioned about your work?
5. Do you often feel anxious?
6. Do you often feel trapped by your career?

If you answer yes to more than a few of these questions, you may be at risk of burning out.

What Can You Do About Burnout?

Here are some ideas I recommend if you're feeling burned out. As a last resort, you may need to change jobs or even switch careers, but be sure to try these other approaches before you do.

- Try substituting one form of stress for another. This may sound like "Out of the frying pan, into the fire," but it works! If your job requires mental concentration, relax with something physical, like jogging or painting your house. If your stress is caused by a boring job—one that doesn't use your intellect—increase your powers of mental concentration by reading, taking a course, or learning a foreign language.

- Try shifting gears to something totally different from work. When I started my doctoral work while working almost a full shift at a veteran's hospital, I began to burn out. Luckily, I happened upon an abandoned Norwegian Elkhound who needed a home. The Dukester and I traveled together for almost 15 years, and no matter how exhausted I was when I came home, she was able to help me put my work behind me.

- Cut back on your excessive hours. Each of us has a limit of effectiveness. After this limit, more time may produce diminishing returns. Sometimes, excessive hours are a condition of employment: law firms and hospitals are notorious for sucking their young employees dry. Often, though, we have a harder time limiting ourselves than we do meeting our boss's expectations.

- Get involved in something bigger than yourself. Try helping out at a homeless shelter or food pantry, a political campaign, or a school.

- Build some solitary time into your life. Take a walk at lunch, go to work a bit earlier, or stay later to ensure that you get some quiet time. Finding solitary time may involve asking somebody, at work or home, to help you out. It's worth the struggle. We all need quiet time to be still and listen to ourselves.

- Give yourself some perks: flowers on a special occasion; a personal day to just take it easy; a new baseball glove or a sewing machine or a camera—something you'll use to have fun.

- Try practicing stress reduction techniques—meditation, deep breathing, and systematic relaxation—in your spare moments.

Take Time Out to Reflect

What is this life if, full of care,
We have no time to stand and stare?

W.H. Davies
Leisure

WHEN I WAS IN FOURTH GRADE, Miss MacNamara called my father and lodged a complaint (not the first, I must admit). "Paul spends too much time daydreaming," she told Dad, who then asked me what I thought I was doing. "I'm not daydreaming, I'm thinking," I said.

There's nothing reprehensible about daydreaming. I think it's greatly underrated, and in this frantic decade in which we live, it's certainly underpracticed. Sometimes we need to stare out the window and just let our minds wander.

If we're always caught up in the battle of the moment, we give short shrift to both the past and the future. I've warned you about the perils of regretting the past and fearing the future, but that doesn't mean that we can't remember what's gone before, and dream of what's ahead. Even people who love their jobs need to take occasional mental breaks from those jobs, and just let the waves break over them.

Our present culture doesn't value solitude and doesn't give us much time alone. Even our solitary commutes to work have been compromised by carpooling, car phones, and self-improvement audiotapes. One busy woman executive told me that she used to find refuge in the bathroom. Now that her children can walk, they barge in on her there too. Her only truly private place is the shower—thankfully, the kids fear the hot water!

Fun Isn't a Four-Letter Word

*There is no duty we so much underrate as
the duty of being happy.*

Robert Louis Stevenson
An Apology for Idlers

SO FEW ADULTS really let themselves have fun.

For most of human history, work and play were not separate. Hunters and gatherers came together into small productive groups—and, later, into organized bands and small cottage industries. Humankind didn't separate home life from work life from social life from personal life. It was all just *life*!

Even today, many aboriginal societies spend only two or three hours per day foraging for food, and the rest of their time napping, chatting, dancing, swimming, making love, telling stories to their children, and relaxing. Not many of us would fully enjoy life in a hut, but the description of aboriginal life does sound a lot like a good vacation: "Club Med—the antidote to civilization!" In early and aboriginal societies, time isn't hurried. To us, time is money. Have we lost something here?

With the emergence of a separate place of work, on the one hand, and the advent of organized Western religion, on the other hand, came the conviction that gratification of the senses was something to postpone, something to hide, or something to eradicate entirely. We've come around to believing that everything that feels good, tastes good, and doesn't produce income is a time-waster or, worse, a danger to us.

Many of us can't even enjoy eating anymore! Today, science has replaced religion as a guide to living. Standards of good and evil have been replaced by standards of healthy and unhealthy. We have come to believe that health arises from the miracle cures of modern medicine, from exercise regimes based on the "no pain, no gain" ethic, and from dietary routines that are, for the most part, pleasure-denying.

In *Healthy Pleasures*,[9] Robert Ornstein and David Sobel explore the healthy effects of pleasure in our lives. Excess is bad, but so is a Spartan life in which you refuse to enjoy good-tasting foods, alcohol, sex, and other pleasures. As Ornstein and Sobel put it, ". . . there is even evidence to suggest that stress and worry about anything—including fats in the diet—can itself raise blood cholesterol levels." Their conclusion: pleasure is good for you.

An Inventory:
What's Really Good for You?

Ornstein and Sobel write: "Healthy pleasures have no side effects and pay off twice: in good feelings and in better health." What pleasurable things are actually good for you?

Touch

Physical touch offers real physical benefits. Premature babies, coma patients, and people in chronic pain all benefit in tangible physical ways from massage, stroking, and cuddling. Massage actually helps release endorphins, your brain's feel-good chemicals.

Scenery

Scenery is good for you too. Hospital patients who can view trees from their beds spend, on average, one fewer day in the hospital than those who don't have a view or have a view of something uninspiring, like a cement wall or a highway.

Music

Music soothes the savage beast, and you too. In one study, one group of premature infants listened to Brahms' *Lullaby*, and one group did not. When the two were compared, it turned out that the Brahms babies gained weight faster. They even left the hospital a week earlier than the other babies—a savings of many thousands of dollars.

Smell

Smell has a good effect on us too. We know from Proust that pleasant smells have a powerful ability to evoke positive memories. Some fragrances have been found to make us more alert; others relax us. In a study of patients suffering chronic pain, the patients were instructed in deep muscle relaxation while they inhaled peach fragrance. Later, simply by inhaling the peach fragrance, the patients induced the relaxation state.

Food

Food isn't the enemy. Certain high-carbohydrate foods, like pasta and cookies, raise brain levels of tryptophan, which helps induce contentment and sleep. Spices like chile peppers thin the blood, aiding in the prevention of heart attacks; they also loosen congestion caused by colds, releasing endorphins as they produce sweat activity and cool the head.

Alcohol

Even alcohol isn't all bad. The coronary arteries of moderate drinkers (those who have one or two drinks a day) are less blocked, and less likely to result in heart disease, than those of either heavy drinkers or those who abstain completely.

Laughter

Laughter can keep us healthy and make us well. When you laugh, you raise your heart rate, stimulate your circulation, and increase your body's production of hormones that relieve pain. In *Anatomy of an Illness as Perceived by the Patient*, Norman Cousins recounts how, after doctors told him he had only months to live, he holed up in a hotel room with *Candid Camera* classics and Marx Brothers films and literally laughed himself well.

And more

Pets, sex, naps, hobbies, and friends all make our lives better—and even, according to recent research, longer.

If anybody objects to all the fun you're having, tell them: "It's doctor's orders!"

Think Beyond Yourself

As far as we can discern, the sole purpose of human existence is to kindle a light in the darkness of mere being.

Carl Gustav Jung
Memories, Dreams, Reflections

EARLY IN MY CAREER as a psychologist, I worked with Vietnam veterans who were struggling to readjust to life in a country that neither understood nor seemed to care about what they'd been through. The physical injuries suffered by these vets were very serious. Though less recognized by society, their psychic wounds were also grave. After I'd worked with the vets for some time, I started to develop a sense of who would make it out of the hospital in a relatively short time, and who would linger there.

Interestingly enough, what most determined when a patient would leave the hospital was not the severity of his injuries, but whether he had a connection to something beyond himself. For some patients, the connection was a family member who needed him at home—a small child who hadn't yet seen her father, a dying parent, a wife who'd been waiting too long. For others, religion served the function. For more than you would imagine, it was a job.

One of my favorite patients was Sean Riley, whose legs had been shattered, then infected during the rehabilitation period. He was in a wheelchair, undergoing both physical and mental therapy, and it looked as if he'd be in the hospital for a long time. As I got to know him and learned his story, I changed my mind. I bet the staff that he'd be one of the first to leave our ward.

Why? He had a real deadline. Sean's elderly father had a small plate glass business that he ran with one helper. The helper was due to retire soon. Unless Sean's dad had help carrying the heavy pieces of plate glass, he would be forced to give up the business; he couldn't cope with hiring an outsider at his age. Sean knew he had to get back on his feet to help his dad keep the business alive.

He did it. Only a few months after we were shaking our heads about his condition, Sean moved to a walker, then to two canes, then to one. Within another month, he walked out of the hospital on his own, and in a few more weeks he was back on the job.

Prevail

I believe man will not merely endure, he will prevail.

William Faulkner
Nobel Prize Acceptance Speech, 1950

TERRIBLE THINGS HAPPEN to the best of people, and somehow they go on to rebuild their lives and their careers.

Sometimes people tell me, "But my situation is different. I can't go on." Mary's husband has abandoned her and left her deeply in debt. Al's wife is dying a slow death from cancer and gradually withdrawing from everyone around her. Ahmad's son is in jail. Paula's mother has Alzheimer's disease. Ben needs to lay off 40 percent of his work force. The painful list goes on and on. Your situation is unique for you, but the reality is that many others have faced similar problems and have found that they can somehow deal with their pain and even go on to work productively again. Support from friends, managers, and coworkers helps immeasurably.

Whenever I hear people's sad stories, I think of Viktor Frankl's *Man's Search for Meaning*, the story of how Dr. Frankl survived more than three years in Auschwitz and other Nazi death camps. It's more than just one more bestial tale of man's inhumanity to man. Dr. Frankl explores why some of his fellow captives survived, and others did not. He observes that those who had a clear purpose, not just a vague hope, survived. He quotes Nietzsche: "He who has a why to live can bear almost any how."

Dr. Frankl takes it a step further:

> *The last of human freedoms ... to choose one's attitude in any given set of circumstances, to choose one's way.*

You don't have the power to control life's events. But you do have the power not to let life's events control you.

Buddy, Can You Spare a Dime?

I must admit that I personally measure success in terms of the contributions an individual makes to his or her fellow human beings.

Margaret Mead
Redbook, 1978

MANY PEOPLE FEEL that they don't have time to give to others. The fact is, you don't have time *not* to! Life is short—for us, but for other people too. Spare a little time to make things better for the people and the world around you. If you give of yourself, you'll be amazed at how much better you'll feel about yourself and the gifts you've been given.

I love the work I do. But during the past few years I've found that my volunteer activities have been as gratifying than anything I've experienced on the job. In the summer of 1991 I was invited to join a group of American executives on a trip to the former Soviet Union. There, we worked one-on-one with local business people, and we organized a mini-business school. The next summer we returned to work intensely on specific projects.

Since the time of these trips, we've given advice about starting businesses and getting funding. Certain people on the trip have helped in specific ways by obtaining computers and other equipment, and putting Eastern European entrepreneurs in touch with marketing and sales people in the West. Some of us have adopted certain local needs as our own; for example, I've tried to raise money in the United States to outfit a children's hospital that was in desperate need of basics we take for granted here. I've made friends I hope to keep for a lifetime, and I've learned as much as I've been able to teach.

There are so many unmet needs for volunteers. Figure out what you can do, in some small niche of the world, that will help make things better. Whether it's a global cause like the Peace Corps or a local cause like your PTA, Town Meeting, or local homeless shelter, see how you can help. Even a few hours and a few dollars can make a difference—to you as well as to those you'll serve.

Give and You Shall Receive

Doing good while doing well.

Ben & Jerry's Ice Cream slogan

ALTRUISM HELPS the giver as much as it helps the receiver. If you need some selfish reasons to give of yourself, here are a few.

If you develop a habit of volunteering while you're still working, you'll be better equipped to deal with retirement—you'll have a ready-made second career. That may be especially important in these days of reductions in force and forced early retirement. A hospital administrator client of mine told me about Fred Barnes, a business executive nearing retirement age who had open heart surgery at his hospital. He ran the hospital volunteers ragged, asking them for water, slippers, and bed cranking, sending them to the lobby newsstand for newspapers and magazines, and begging them (unsuccessfully) for contraband snacks from the cafeteria. He came to value the efforts of these aides, and he resolved that if he recovered, he'd become a volunteer himself. Fred kept his pledge, and despite business pressures when he returned to work, he does regular shifts at the hospital and plans to do even more once he's retired.

When Jimmy Carter was unceremoniously retired from the Presidency, he and Rosalynn went back to Plains, Georgia and swore to do more with their remaining years than give speeches, sit on boards, and go to banquets. Did they ever! Through Habitat for Humanity, they've built houses for the needy, and through the Carter Center, they've mediated crises around the world. Their book, *Everything To Gain: Making the Most of the Rest of Your Life*, is a wonderful guide to how you can use your retirement years to change both your life and your world.

Volunteerism makes you feel better about yourself, and because you do feel better about yourself, you'll find that you work more effectively. One of Boston's leading management recruiters, John Sullivan, has many business and family responsibilities, yet he finds time to run a support group for the unemployed. When I ask him how he does it, he shrugs and says, "Well, I'm tired when I get there. When I leave, I'm still tired, but I feel better."

Altruism may even save your life. People speak of the "special glow" they feel when they help a friend, a neighbor, or a stranger in need. Studies show that the glow may even be a physical one. People who volunteer regularly are only half as likely to suffer strokes and heart attacks as those who don't. And, those who do have strokes and heart attacks recover more quickly.[9]

Be a Mentor

No man is an Island, entire of itself; every man is a piece of the continent, a part of the main. If a clod be washed away by the sea, Europe is the less, as well as if a promontory were, as well as if a manor of thy friends or of thine own were. Any man's death diminishes me, because I am involved in Mankind, and therefore never send to know for whom the bell tolls, it tolls for thee.

John Donne
XVII—Meditation

THERE'S PLENTY OF ROOM for altruism in your professional life. Did someone help you when you were looking for a job or getting a start in your career? Return the favor. Be a mentor yourself.

Some colleges and technical/vocational schools offer mentoring programs that allow students who are interested in certain careers to work one term or one summer with someone who actually has that career. Other mentoring programs may be more limited; they allow students to conduct interviews and call their mentors from time to time for information and guidance. Do you wish that you'd had more guidance back when you got started in a job or switched careers? Do for someone else what you wish someone had done for you. Help someone who works for you learn more skills. Push them along.

There's another really easy way to share yourself at work. Give some praise. It's free and it's amazingly valuable. When's the last time anyone turned to you and said, "You know, you do a great job. I really appreciate it." Say it to someone else. Make their day.

One Person Can Make a Difference

Am I my brother's keeper?

Gen. 4:9

OFTEN, although we want to give something back to our world, we're hesitant to try. We're stretched for time. Or we're so boggled by the size and complexity of the problems around us that we feel that our tiny contribution can't make a dent. If your dream is to patch the ozone layer, to cure AIDS, or to feed the hungry, you'll learn quickly that wishing doesn't make it so. No matter how much you care, or how hard you work each day, the problem will be sitting there the next day, maybe looming even larger.

Barbara Penn, a social worker for the Massachusetts Department of Social Services (DSS), cared deeply about the abused children she worked with, but she was losing hope. "No matter what we do to help, no matter how hard we work," she said, "every year there are more abused kids. We're just not winning." Barbara felt that every day she contributed to saving lives and putting families back together. But the dimensions of the total problem were just too daunting psychologically.

When we met, Barbara was considering a job change. She faced the unpleasant fact that in most business jobs she'd be at an entry level. And she acknowledged that she wasn't very enthusiastic about business work, so we turned to trying to improve her existing job situation. She was already working as hard as she could. We tried to think strategically about how Barbara could leverage her skills and her caring. Here are some concrete moves she decided to make:

- She got more involved with her professional organization. She learned about legislative activities affecting DSS, and she focused attention on ways of persuading the legislature to fund new and promising programs.

- Through her professional organization, she consulted with social workers in a master's program who were wrestling with career choices of their own.

- She agreed to teach an evening course for college-age students interested in social work as a profession.

Barbara felt challenged by her new activities. She also felt that she was touching the lives of people who would ultimately save more children than she had a hope of saving on her own.

A Lot Is Better than a Little, But a Little Is Better than Nothing

Nobody makes a greater mistake than he who does nothing because he could only do a little.

Edmund Burke

WE'VE URGED YOU to dream a big dream and shoot for the stars. But sometimes, you can't blaze into a new world without looking back. Many people who want to make a change, or feel uncomfortable with their current choice of profession or job, find themselves stuck. They're convinced that they've got to either stay right where they are, without changing a thing, or throw it all over and start fresh. They forget that compromise is possible.

Rebecca Cutler is Vice-President of Public Relations in a growing technology company. She likes the excitement of her job and the income that goes along with it. As the years go rolling by, however, she has begun to feel guilty about using her talents strictly for herself. She'd like to give something back to the community, and she thinks she might find it personally rewarding to work with autistic children through a social service organization.

Rebecca had been wrestling with what seemed to her to be a black and white choice: satisfaction or compensation. But, when she finally took a step back from the situation and tried to find a compromise, she realized that she could begin by doing volunteer work with autistic children. She'd get the satisfaction that goes with that work, but not have to give up completely her challenging and high-paying PR job. Long-term, she's working on deciding how satisfying and successful her work with the children will be. She's also looking, in a business-like way, at the problem of autism: How is it treated? Is there anything new, from a treatment or technological point of view? How are prevention and treatment organizations funded and structured? Ultimately, she hopes to work full-time in the treatment of autism, but she is hoping to find a way to do this without giving up completely on earning the money she feels she's worth.

There is a bumper sticker that's very popular in my area of the country: "Think globally, act locally." That's a thought I like. Sometimes it makes sense for us to work in a small, local way, within the context of our current lives, towards a global or long-term goal.

Put It in Perspective

For what shall it profit a man,
if he shall gain the whole world
and lose his own soul?

Mark 8:36

I WANT YOU TO LOVE your work and feel that the many years of your life you devote to working pay off. But some things are more important than work: family, health, friends. These are the pieces of your life that will keep you going if you lose your job, if illness strikes your family, if a hurricane destroys your home. We've all heard St. Mark's admonition, and a lot of lesser folks have echoed his sentiments. But we keep forgetting. We keep letting our jobs get to us, we come home cranky, and we don't make time—or emotional space—for our families and other attachments and for the various communities that engage us.

At some level, you've got to be ready and willing to lose worldly things and save your soul—whether you mean something religious by that is up to you. A person who knows what's important, and can be sustained by what's important, can always put a plan together to regain material things. (In fact, many millionaires report that they made and lost a million dollars two or three times before they managed to hang onto one.) It's a lot harder to win back a family's trust or a friend's belief in you.

Giving your all to a job sometimes means just that. You may feel there's nothing left to give to anyone or anything else. But if you don't give, then eventually the people and institutions around you will stop asking you to share yourself with them. That will be the time that you realize how much you've lost. Hard as it is to make time for everything, you've got to try.

The best jobs in the world can't shield you from pain and human need. George Bush lost a child, Donald Trump lost his marriage. Their great successes couldn't keep them from feeling the pain of human loss. Value what you have beyond your job— and give these other people and causes the attention they deserve.

There Are Many Kinds of Dreams

The future belongs to those who believe in the beauty of their dreams.

Eleanor Roosevelt

OUR DREAMS OF SUCCESS don't always have to focus on our work. Our children and our community activities can fulfill us too.

Self-fulfillment is a wonderful goal. But for some people, and in some phases of life, working towards the fulfillment of others may be a wholly satisfactory activity. Parents who can afford to stay home to nurture children full-time, or those who work in less than challenging jobs while they find their fullest enjoyment in home or community or educational activities—these people can also love what they do, and should be able to feel guilt-free about being fulfilled by the mix of activities that makes their lives worthwhile.

At a workshop I presented to the University of Massachusetts Alumni Association, one participant—a restaurant manager—brought tears to the eyes of a number of people in the audience by telling the story of one of his employees. Vath Soon was a refugee who had escaped from the atrocities in Cambodia and found a new life in America, washing dishes in a restaurant kitchen. He brought up five children the best he knew how, and he taught them all to dream. One of his daughters became a doctor and the other a lawyer. His three sons grew up to be a doctor, a lawyer, and an accountant. He's still washing dishes, but with a big smile on his face. His big dream—his dream of his children's success—came true.

An Exercise in Deciding What's Important

In a moment of quiet reflection, ask yourself:

1. What are truly the most important things in my life?

   Most of us will say that the most important things are our family—spouse or partner, children, parents, friends—both old and new, our health, and perhaps our community, social, and religious affiliations.

2. What have I done lately to nurture or protect them?

   So often, we make little time for the people who we say are most important to us.

3. What active steps do I need to take right now?

   Resolve to give one extra hour a week of single-minded attention to each of your children. Next time you see an old friend, ask what's on his or her mind, instead of plunging into a recital of what's new with you. Make that medical appointment and start a realistic exercise program. Cherish what's important.

Can You Have It All?

You can't always get what you want
But if you try, sometimes you'll get what you need.

Keith Richards and Mick Jagger
You Can't Always Get What You Want

SOMETIMES we *can't* have it all.

Eric Baxter found this out when he accepted a promotion and moved from Boston to start up the new West Coast office of the ad agency he'd worked at for many years. Because his wife had a good job in Boston, and his two children were still in school, the family agreed that he would move alone and the rest of the family would join him eight months later, at the end of the school year. Eric tried commuting back and forth once or twice a month, but he found himself exhausted from the demands of the new job. His wife found herself overwhelmed by the new demands of single parenthood and deeply saddened about leaving her own job. And the children suffered the most. One became very depressed, and the other started to act up in school.

After several months, when Eric's family looked at the new situation objectively, they found that nobody was winning. Even Eric, who had been thrilled with the new job, was unhappy. He decided the additional money and status weren't worth the pain, and he asked to be reassigned back to Boston after he'd been able to train a replacement. His company was unexpectedly understanding, and Eric and his family were able to salvage a bad situation.

We can't always reverse a bad decision this way. Before you jump into a new situation—a new career, a new job, an increased work load, a new project requiring lots of travel—take the time to look at all the other parts of your life, and make sure you understand how they'll be affected by the new demands. Sometimes, given the requirements of your profession or the realities of the economy, you won't have the luxury of refusing an assignment. But be sure you take the time at least to consider, and prepare for, the consequences.

Put the Pieces Together

*We traditionally have set up a dualism between work and
life as if one is not part of the other.*

James A. Autry,
letter to Paul Powers, October 29, 1990

THIS BOOK MAY STRIKE YOU as an odd blend of workaday hints and
life lessons. There's a reason for this. Too many of us split our lives in two—work on
one side, life on the other. I believe that work is too important to our hearts and
souls to be cut off from "life." And I believe that our personal qualities and dreams
are too much a part of ourselves to be checked at the office door. So often, if you
love your work, you'll love your life. Work is vital to making us what we are.

I like the way the chairman of the board (played by Gregory Peck) puts it in the 1991
movie, *Other People's Money:*

> *A business . . . is the place where we earn our living, where we meet our
> friends, and dream our dreams. It is, in every sense, the very fabric that
> binds our society together.*

With the permission of James A. Autry, a business executive and the author of *Love
and Profit: The Art of Caring Leadership*, I'm including the concluding lines from his
poem, "Threads," which beautifully expresses the mix of work and life I think is so
important.

> *In every office*
> *you hear the threads*
> *of love and joy and fear and guilt,*
> *the cries for celebration and reassurance,*
> *and somehow you know that connecting those*
> *threads*
> *is what you are supposed to do*
> *and business takes care of itself.*

For Further Reading

In this section we've collected references to books and studies cited throughout *Love Your Job!*, as well as some additional source books you'll find helpful as you ponder your next step.

Notes

The following notes briefly summarize the sources for research cited in this book.

1. The study by Dr. Peter L. Schnall of Cornell University Medical College, NY, was reported in Lindsey Tanner, "Job Stress Linked To Heart Woes," Associated Press story, April, 1990. The study was originally published in the *Journal of the American Medical Association*. In this particular study, 215 men, ages 30-60, were studied at seven work sites in New York (including stock brokerages, private hospitals, and garbage collection facilities). Schnall found that job stress was "significantly related" to heart risks after adjusting for such factors as age, alcohol intake, and smoking.

   A variety of new studies, drawing from international research on work and stress, appear in the January, 1993 *Conditions of Work Digest*. Early studies on job enjoyment and stress are reported in Harry Levinson, *Executive Stress*, Harper & Row Publishers, New York, NY, 1970, and in Lawrence Galton, *Coping With Executive Stress*, McGraw-Hill Publishing Company, New York, NY, 1973.

2. Frederick Herzberg's research is reported in his books, *Work and the Nature of Man* and *The Motivation to Work*, and in "One More Time: How Do You Motivate Employees?" *Harvard Business Review*, Boston, MA, September-October, 1987, Reprint #87507.

3. In *Divorcing a Corporation*, Dr. Jacqueline Hornor Plumez divides work "assets" into seven main categories: quality of an organization, work environment, money, growth, interpersonal relations, lifestyle, and job content. Dr. Stephen Bishop's unpublished research into reasons why people enjoy their jobs is also of great interest in this area.

4. Edgar H. Schein has written a booklet containing a questionnaire and interview aimed at detecting your "career anchors." *Career Anchors: Discovering Your Real Values*, Pfeiffer & Company, San Diego, CA, 1990, is based on his research, originally reported in E. H. Schein, *Career Dynamics: Matching Individual and Organizational Needs*, Addison-Wesley Publishing Company, Reading, MA, 1978, and E. H. Schein, "Individuals and Careers" in J. Lorsch (ed.), *Handbook of Organizational Behavior*, Prentice-Hall, Englewood Cliffs, NJ, 1985.

5. Dr. Martha Friedman's research, recounted in *Overcoming the Fear of Success*, looks at the unconscious roadblocks people set up to success both in their careers and in their personal lives. She looks at the childhood roots of fear of success and explores ways people can overcome their fears. Unfortunately, Dr. Friedman's book is now out of print, but it is available in many libraries.

6. Dr. Mihaly Csikszentmihalyi's research isn't limited to managers in the industrialized world, the way so much workplace research is. In *Flow: The Psychology of Optimal Experience*, he recounts studies of Navajo shepherds, farmers in the Italian Alps, workers on a Chicago assembly line, elderly women in Korea, adults in Thailand and India, and teenagers in Tokyo.

7. Dr. Martin E.P. Seligman's research into optimism is described in *Learned Optimism*. He also cites the groundbreaking contributions by Albert Ellis, in *Reason and Emotion in Psychotherapy*, Stuart, New York, NY, 1962, and A.T. Beck in A.T. Beck, A.J. Rush, B.F. Shaw, and G. Emery, *Cognitive Therapy of Depression: A Treatment Manual*, Guilford, New York, NY, 1979.

8. The Holmes-Rahe Life Event-Stress Scale, devised by Thomas H. Holmes and R.H. Rahe, was originally published as "The Social Readjustment Rating Scale," *Journal of Psychosomatic Research*, 11: pp. 213-218, Pergamon Press, Oxford, England, 1967. It also appears in Lawrence Galton, *Coping With Executive Stress*, McGraw Hill Publishing Company, New York, NY, 1973.

9. In *Healthy Pleasures*, Dr. Robert Ornstein and Dr. David Sobel explore the benefits of pleasure, both in immediate enjoyment and in long-term health. They cite a number of sources for information about the physical benefits of altruism, including:

J.S. House, C. Robbins, and H.L. Metzner,
"The Association of Social Relationships and Activities with Mortality," *American Journal of Epidemiology*, 116: pp. 123-140, 1982.

D. Hurley, "Getting Help from Helping,"
Psychology Today, 22(1): pp. 63-67, January, 1988.

A. Kohn, "Beyond Selfishness,"
Psychology Today, 22(10): pp. 34-38, October, 1988.

A. Luks, "Helper's High,"
Psychology Today, 22(10): pp. 39-42, October, 1988.

A. Luks and E. Growald
American Health, March, 1988.

Job Hunting Guides

There are many books out there that purport to help you write a winning resumé, bowl them over in an interview, and write inquiry letters that will win hearts and jobs. Some are good and some are not so good. These are the books the people I counsel have found to be the most useful.

Beatty, Richard H., *The Complete Job Search Book*, John Wiley & Sons, New York, NY, 1988.

> This book focuses on resumé preparation, but also touches on direct mail, interviewing, and negotiation. Two highlights of this book are the sections on networking and on selecting the employer whose environment and culture are right for you.

Bolles, Richard Nelson, *What Color Is Your Parachute?*, Ten Speed Press, Berkeley, CA, 1992.

> This classic is updated annually to reflect new information and readers' suggestions. It's an entertaining and inspiring work that contains a lot of basic advice for the new job hunter, strong sections on skills inventories and taking a systematic approach to the job hunt, and an excellent reference section for directories, associations, and resources for job hunters with special needs.

Burton, Mary Lindley and Wedemeyer, Richard A., *In Transition*, HarperCollins Publishers, New York, NY, 1991.

> Based on the popular Harvard Business School Club of New York's Career Management Seminar, this book is aimed at the professional manager who is out of work. It takes a rigorous and carefully paced approach to examining your skills and interests, and finding the job that suits you. It includes such suggestions as putting together a "Board of Directors" to help you in your job search.

Germann, Richard, Bleumenson, Diane, and Arnold, Peter, *Working and Liking It*, Fawcett-Columbine Books, New York, NY, 1984.

> This book is "an owner's manual for your job." It focuses on how you can repair problems in your job, set and meet appropriate goals, and conduct a job search within your own corporation.

Greco, Ben, *How To Get the Job That's Right for You*, Dow Jones-Irwin, Homewood, IL, 1980.

> Greco's book has a lot of sound information about career decision strategy and contains some useful forms for personal inventories and employer ratings. It's particularly helpful if you have a clear job goal and you're looking for help in putting a strategy together.

Jackson, Tom, *Guerilla Tactics in the New Job Market*, Bantam Books, New York, NY, 1991 (second edition).

> This book focuses on targeting employers and jobs that are right for you, takes a look at planning for the future, and contains some solid information on resumés and interviewing. This book is as useful for the person who wants to advance in his or her career from within as it is for the job hunter. It's full of anecdotes and helpful tactics.

Leeds, Dorothy, *Marketing Yourself*, HarperCollins Publishers, New York, NY, 1991.

> Taking a sales and marketing approach, this book focuses on knowing your market, selling yourself to an employer, and closing the sale. It also focuses on ten "success factors"— the most marketable skills that get people hired.

Yate, Martin John, *Knock 'em Dead with Great Answers to Tough Interview Questions*, Bob Adams Publishers, Holbrook, MA, 1992.

> If you're only going to read one book on interviewing, this is it. It contains a general discussion about job hunting, cold calling, and writing your resumé and "executive briefing." The meat of the book is the more than 150 questions and suggested answers to interviewers' questions. See also Yate's related books: *Resumés That Knock 'em Dead* and *Cover Letters That Knock 'em Dead*.

Other Recommended Books

The books in this section are a mishmash of books that have inspired me personally. Some have a business slant, others are directed more towards self-analysis and personal development. All have a lot to offer.

Autry, James A., *Love and Profit: The Art of Caring Leadership*, William Morrow and Company, New York, NY, 1991.

> Autry is a seasoned Fortune 500 executive and an accomplished poet. In this volume he blends his two special talents to describe a workplace in which both achievement and people matter.

Blanchard, Kenneth and Johnson, Spencer, *The One-Minute Manager*, William Morrow and Company, New York, NY, 1981.

> This book is a quick, easy to understand parable about how to apply basic behavioral psychology to organizational life through one-minute goals, one-minute praisings, and one-minute reprimands.

Byham, William with Cox, Jeff, *Zapp: The Lightning of Empowerment*, Fawcett-Columbine Books, New York, NY, 1992.

> A fable about employee empowerment, in somewhat the style of *The One-Minute Manager*. In the tale, employees learn the difference between "sapping" people, which discourages them, and "zapping" them, which energizes them and makes them happier and more productive.

Carlzon, Jan, *Moments of Truth*, HarperCollins Publishers, New York, NY, 1987.

> There are certain moments that define us as people and organizations. This book, by the CEO of Scandinavian Airlines (SAS), illuminates such moments by looking at several business turnarounds. Carlzon's approach to customer-driven management involves principles of individual freedom and responsibility, risk-taking, and good communication.

Carnegie, Dale, *How To Win Friends and Influence People*, revised edition with Carnegie, Dorothy and Pell, Arthur R., Pocket Books, New York, NY, 1982 (originally published by Simon and Schuster, 1936).

> Dale Carnegie is the grandfather of the human relations movement. Although somewhat dated, this book is a fount of wisdom about managing the "people" element of your job and career in a humane and productive way. Interestingly, this is the one Western "management" book that many managers in the former Soviet Union know and respect.

Carter, Jimmy and Carter, Rosalynn, *Everything to Gain: Making the Most of the Rest of Your Life*, Random House, New York, NY, 1987.

> The Carters write, in two voices, about how the retirement years can be used productively and altruistically. An appendix lists the addresses and telephone numbers of 52 organizations that need your help and energy, including the Carters' own special cause, Habitat for Humanity, 419 West Church Street, Americus, GA, 31709, (912) 924-6935.

Cousins, Norman, *Anatomy of an Illness as Perceived by the Patient*, W.W. Norton & Company, New York, NY, 1979.

> This book recounts Cousins' own experience with a serious disease of the connective tissue. It explores his theory of how positive emotions, such as faith, love, and laughter, can produce positive chemical changes, and it discusses how he he fought off an apparently hopeless diagnosis with vitamins and plenty of laughter.

Cousins, Norman, *Head First: The Biology of Hope*, E.P. Dutton, New York, NY, 1989.

> This book builds on Cousins' previous book, providing a wealth of scientific evidence for his conviction that the mind can help mobilize the body's healing resources. Much of the work is based on Cousins' research and diagnostic experiences as adjunct professor and researcher at UCLA School of Medicine.

Covey, Stephen R., *The Seven Habits of Highly Effective People*, Fireside Books, Simon and Schuster, New York, NY, 1989.

> This book looks at the "habits" or principles that help us solve both personal and professional problems. Covey's advice is to 1) be proactive; 2) begin with the end in mind; 3) put first things first; 4) think win-win; 5) seek first to understand, then to be understood; 6) synergize; and 7) sharpen the saw.

Crosby, Faye J., *Juggling*, The Free Press, division of Macmillan Company, New York, NY, 1991.

> This book looks at the "juggling" that so many contemporary women do—balancing home, children, work, and other involvements, and at the guilt and stress they so often feel. Sifting through a large body of research, Crosby finds that there are unexpected advantages in such juggling to both women and their families.

Csikszentmihalyi, Mihaly, *Flow: The Psychology of Optimal Experience*, HarperCollins Publishers, New York, NY, 1990.

> This book contains research on workers in a wide range of cultures and occupations. Csikszentmihalyi's thesis is that job dissatisfaction almost always stems from either anxiety or boredom. "Flow" is the feeling of satisfaction people feel when they love what they are doing. Although this is a rather technical book, working your way through it will bring ample rewards.

Deal, Terrence E. and Kennedy, Allen A., *Corporate Cultures: The Rites and Rituals of Corporate Life*, Addison-Wesley Publishing Company, Reading, MA, 1982.

> This is the book that made the term, "corporate culture," a permanent part of the management lexicon. Deal and Kennedy explore what a company's environment, or culture, means to an organization and its employees, look at problems among organizations and workers, and help answer the question: How can you figure out what type of organization is right for you?

Ellis, Albert and Harper, Robert, *A New Guide to Rational Living*, Wilshire Books, Prentice-Hall, Englewood Cliffs, NJ, 1975 (originally published as *A Guide to Rational Living*, Wilshire Books, 1955).

> A good introductory volume by the father of rational emotive therapy (RET). Ellis argues that rational thinking is the quickest route to mental health and self-acceptance. He says that rather than blaming other people or past history for our problems, we can achieve satisfaction by accepting what is going on in the world as reality, being flexible in our thinking, and setting appropriate goals.

Frankl, Viktor, *Man's Search for Meaning*, Pocket Books, division of Simon and Schuster, New York, NY, 1976 (originally published by Beacon Press, 1959).

> Viktor Frankl is an eminent psychiatrist who was imprisoned for years in Nazi concentration camps. This book is a stirring memoir of those years and an exposition of his belief that people can survive the most hopeless situations if they have some purpose in doing so.

Friedman, Martha, *Overcoming the Fear of Success*, Seaview Books, division of HarperCollins Publishers, New York, NY, 1980.

> Although it's less often recognized, almost as many people fear success as fear failure. How can you detect this fear in yourself and overcome it? This book is a wonderful collection of stories and practical suggestions.

Gardner, Howard, *Frames of Mind*, BasicBooks, division of HarperCollins Publishers, New York, NY, 1985.

> Gardner points out the fallacy of measuring all types of people and skills with a single, linguistically-oriented measure of intelligence and explores the "theory of multiple intelligences." This theory provides a means of assessing and appreciating levels of competence in wide-ranging skills, including writing, navigation, music, and sports. The book defines seven main "intelligences": 1) linguistic; 2) musical; 3) logical-mathematical; 4) spatial; 5) bodily-kinesthetic; 6) intrapersonal; and 7) interpersonal.

Herzberg, Frederick, *Work and the Nature of Man*, The World Publishing Company, Cleveland, OH, 1966.

> This book is rather technical, but it contains interesting material about the meaning of work in our lives and the factors that motivate us to work productively and enthusiastically.

Hyatt, Carole, *Shifting Gears*, Simon and Schuster, New York, NY, 1990.

> This book focuses on changing careers in mid-life and how to find the work that's right for you. It looks at the results of 300 interviews, presents the notion of "trigger points" in life, and develops a program for personal change and work style.

Iacocca, Lee with Novak, William, *Iacocca*, Bantam Books, New York, NY, 1984.

> This is an inspiring story of an immigrant's son who rose to become the successful and charismatic CEO of a major U.S. corporation and the spokesman for American industrial policy. Among other things, he points out that getting fired can be the best thing for your career.

Mackay, Harvey, *Beware the Naked Man Who Offers You His Shirt*, Ballantine Books, New York, NY, 1990.

> The CEO of the Mackay Envelope Corporation and the author of *Swim With The Sharks Without Getting Eaten Alive*, *Sharkproof*, and several other books, Harvey Mackay has put together a collection of vignettes—some humorous, some inspirational—containing advice about doing what you love, loving what you do, and delivering more than you promise.

Naisbitt, John and Aburdene, Patricia, *Megatrends 2000: Ten New Directions for the 1990s*, William Morrow and Company, New York, NY, 1990.

> The prophetic authors of *Megatrends* take a humanistic look at the 1990s and see ten new trends: 1) global economic boom; 2) renaissance in the arts; 3) emergence of free market socialism; 4) global lifestyles and cultural nationalism; 5) privatization of the welfare state; 6) rise of the Pacific Rim; 7) decade of women in leadership; 8) age of biology; 9) religious revival of the Third Millenium; and 10) triumph of the individual.

Ornstein, Robert and Sobel, David, *Healthy Pleasures*, Addison-Wesley Publishing Company, Reading, MA, 1989.

> This book makes the point that pleasures are good for you—touch, music, smell, food, even alcohol in moderation. Research shows that these pleasures, and others, actually produce positive physical benefits.

Peale, Norman Vincent, *The Power of Positive Thinking*, Fawcett Crest Books, Ballantine Books, New York, NY, 1984 (originally published by Prentice-Hall, 1952).

This inspirational work is a classic and remains one of the best in the field of personal development. It has a somewhat religious emphasis, but you don't need to be a religious person to benefit from Peale's thinking on creating energy and happiness, expecting the best, defeating worry, using faith, and getting people to like you.

Plumez, Jacqueline Hornor with Dougherty, Karla, *Divorcing a Corporation*, Villard Books, New York, NY, 1986.

This book looks at the corporation as our surrogate family and explores how hard it is to break the family tie, even when a job isn't right for us. Plumez analyzes the "golden handcuffs" that keep us in jobs, the reasons why our work satisfies or doesn't satisfy us, and the ways we can determine when and how to leave the corporate "family."

Schuller, Robert H., *Tough Times Never Last, but Tough People Do*, Bantam Books, New York, NY, 1984.

This book also has a religious emphasis. Schuller points to spiritual faith and prayer as a means of putting your problems in proper perspective and taking charge of your life.

Seligman, Martin E.P., *Learned Optimism,* Alfred A. Knopf Publishers, New York, NY, 1990.

This book puts the weight of modern psychological research behind traditional theories of the power of positive thinking and attitude management. Time and time again, Seligman finds that optimists do better—in school, at work, with their health, in sports, in politics, and at home. Through techniques explained in this book, people can unlearn passivity and helplessness and can learn to be happier and to expect better of themselves and their world.

Sher, Barbara, with Gottlieb, Annie, *Wishcraft: How to Get What You Really Want*, Ballantine Books, New York, NY, 1979.

This book describes effective strategies for making real changes in your life. It helps put vague yearnings and dreams to work, with concrete results.

Siegel, Bernie, *Love, Medicine, and Miracles*, HarperCollins Publishers, New York, NY, 1986.

Along the same lines as Norman Cousins' books, this book looks at those who suffer chronic illnesses and those who have survived illnesses thought to be terminal. Recoveries cannot always be explained by modern medicine.

Sinetar, Marsha, *Do What You Love, The Money Will Follow*, Dell Publishing, New York, NY, 1987.

> This inspirational guide shows you the way to finding the work that expresses who you are and what you love and that lets you grow to be a better person through your work.

Terkel, Studs, *Working*, **Pantheon Books, division of Random House, New York, NY, 1972.**

> Terkel's wonderful oral narratives of working people, ranging from farmers to publishers, washroom attendants to jockeys, pharmacists to bus drivers, paint a vivid picture of work that is loved and work that is hated.

Tieger, Paul D. and Barron-Tieger, Barbara, *Do What You Are*, Little, Brown and Company, Boston, MA, 1992.

> An interesting guide, filled with real-life examples illustrating the connection between personality type and career satisfaction.

Directories

When you're trying to figure out where and even what the jobs are, you'll find these directories useful. Most large libraries have them.

Company Information: Public and Private

Dun & Bradstreet's Million Dollar Directory, Dun's Marketing Services, 3 Sylvan Way, Parsippany, NJ, 07054.

> An annual 3-volume publication containing more than 13,000 pages of information on 140,000 U.S. companies with net worths of $1,000,000 and more. Information is organized in three separate ways: alphabetically by company name, geographically by state, and functionally by Standard Industry Code (SIC) (industrial classification). Each entry lists company address, officer names, products, sales, and number of employees.

Dun & Bradstreet's Middle Market Directory, Dun's Marketing Services, 3 Sylvan Way, Parsippany, NJ, 07054.

> Contains the same information (as above) for U.S. companies with a net worth between $500,000 and $1,000,000.

Dun & Bradstreet's Business Information Reports, Dun's Marketing Services, 3 Sylvan Way, Parsippany, NJ, 07054.

> Contains comprehensive and in-depth information about private companies.

Dun & Bradstreet's Reference Book of Corporate Management, Dun's Marketing Services, 3 Sylvan Way, Parsippany, NJ, 07054.

> Contains a list of key executives for 3000 companies, arranged alphabetically by company (3500 pages in four volumes).

MacRae's State Industrial Directories, MacRae's Blue Book, Inc., Plainview, NY, 11803.

> There is one book for each state, representing a total of 50,000 companies. All companies are listed in three separate ways: alphabetically by company name, geographically by state, and functionally by Standard Industry Code (SIC) (industrial classification). The book lists parent companies, as well as subsidiaries and divisions.

Thomas Register of American Manufacturers, Thomas Publishing Company, 1 Penn Plaza, New York, NY, 10001.

> An annual 21-volume publication containing 30,000 pages of information. Volumes 1-11 list firms by product; volume 12 contains an index to products and services; volume 13 contains company profiles; volume 14 contains an index by

product trade names; and volumes 15-21 contain the catalogs of more than 1200 manufacturing firms.

For Public Companies Only

Moody's Manuals, Dun & Bradstreet, 99 Church Street, New York, NY, 10007.

> An annual publication, with semi-weekly supplements. There are seven separate books: *Bank and Finance, Industrial, OTC Industrial, Municipal and Government, Public Utilities, Transportation, and International*. The information includes a history of the companies and their operations, subsidiaries, plants, products, officers and directors, comparative income statements, balance sheet, selected financial ratios, and description of outstanding securities.

Standard Corporation Records, Standard & Poor's Corporation, 25 Broadway, New York, NY, 10004.

> A looseleaf, bimonthly publication with daily supplements. In addition to the information in Moody's, this publication contains a Daily News section, which is a good source of up-to-date information on public companies.

Standard & Poor's Register of Corporations, Directors, and Executives, Standard & Poor's Corporation, 25 Broadway, New York, NY, 10004.

> A 3-volume publication. Volume 1 lists major companies by industry and geography; volume 2 contains detailed information on the companies; and volume 3 contains personal data on many executives.

For Locating News Articles About a Company or an Industry

F&S Index of Corporations and Industries. Predicasts, Inc., Cleveland, OH, 44101.

> A weekly publication with cumulative indexes of articles appearing in more than 750 publications, including trade journals. Information is arranged by company name and SIC code.

Reader's Guide to Periodical Literature: Business Periodicals Index

> A guide to articles about businesses and business news.

There are also guides available for articles in specific large newspapers, including:

Wall Street Journal Index

New York Times Index

Chicago Tribune Index

Los Angeles Times Index

Washington Post Index

Government Publications

Dictionary of Occupational Titles, Bureau of Labor Statistics, U.S. Department of Labor, 441 G Street N.W., Washington, DC. 20212.

> A publication containing one page for each occupational title you might encounter while reading the want ads, working with headhunters, etc.

Occupational Outlook Handbook, Bureau of Labor Statistics, U.S. Department of Labor, 441 G Street N.W., Washington, DC. 20212.

> A publication that explores job titles in more detail and contains information on past and projected employment figures and salary surveys by industry and geography.

Standard Industrial Classification Manual, Bureau of Labor Statistics, 441 G Street N.W., Washington, DC. 20212.

> A publication showing the widely used standard industrial classifications (4-digit SIC codes). This manual is not updated frequently, so recent occupations are not listed.

Company Publications

For information about a specific company or the companies in a particular community, consider the following:

- Annual reports of companies are an excellent source of information about the people, products, and finances of organizations.

- To find out more about a particular local company, check with the local Better Business Bureau and Chamber of Commerce.

- The want ads are an excellent source of information about who's in a community, who's hiring (even if it's not in your functional area—yet), and what products they're developing, marketing, or supporting.

- Even your local Yellow Pages, particularly the Business-to-Business version, is a source of basic information about who does what.

- Stockbrokers can be an excellent source of information about what companies do and what their finances are—if you have one, ask for information.

- Go straight to the horse's mouth. Call the company's marketing department and ask them to send you a package of information about the company and its products or services.

- If you have a personal friend or acquaintance in an organization, ask them to get copies of any internal publications (e.g., newsletters, press releases, product information bulletins) they're allowed to share.

Other Useful Directories

Contacts Influential: Commerce and Industry Directory

A guide to businesses in particular markets. There's one volume for each major city or area of the country. Includes names, type of business, key personnel, etc., for 150 key areas.

Directory of Directories, Gale Research Inc., Book Tower, Detroit, MI, 48226.

A 2-volume directory to all the other directories out there. Lists, among other things, sources of information about particular industries. Contains more than 10,000 entries, as well as a title, subject, and keyword index.

Directory of Executive Recruiters, Kennedy & Kennedy, Inc., Fitzwilliam, NH 03447.

This directory lists the top 2000 recruiters doing business in the U.S. Mailing labels may be purchased from Kennedy & Kennedy.

Directory of Outplacement Firms, Kennedy & Kennedy, Inc., Fitzwilliam, NH 03447.

This directory lists the top outplacement firms. Labels are also available.

Encyclopedia of Associations, Gale Research Inc., Book Tower, Detroit, MI, 48226.

Volume 1 of this publication contains a guide to U.S. professional societies, trade associations, and interest groups, including the names of executive directors. Volume 2 contains business organizations and their publications.

Encyclopedia of Associations, International Organizations, Gale Research Inc., Book Tower, Detroit, MI, 48226.

A guide to international organizations and national organizations based outside the United States.

Levine, Michael, *The Address Book: How to Reach Anyone Who Is Anyone*, Perigee Book, The Putnam Publishing Group, New York, NY, 10016.

This frequently updated book contains addresses and telephone numbers for 3500 politicians, business people, people in the arts, and other movers and shakers.

WE'D LIKE TO HEAR FROM YOU

If you have comments about this book or a story about a job you love (or hate), please share it (and let us know if we can include it in the next edition of this book). If you have a favorite quotation you'd like us to include in this or future books, please send that as well. *—Dr. Paul Powers & Deborah Russell*

LOVE
—your—
JOB!

Name _____ Company Name (optional)

Address _____

City/State _____ Zip/Country

Telephone _____ FAX _____ E-mail Address (Internet or Uunet)

WE'D LIKE TO HEAR FROM YOU

If you'd like any of the following, please check the appropriate box and return:

- ❏ Information on discounts for orders of ten or more copies of this book.

- ❏ Information about *Love Your Job!* seminars or human resources consulting services for my organization.

LOVE
—your—
JOB!

- ❏ Information about having Dr. Paul Powers speak at my professional group's meeting or conference.

- ❏ A list of O'Reilly book distributors outside the U.S. and Canada.

Name _____ Company Name (optional)

Address _____

City/State _____ Zip/Country

Telephone _____ FAX _____ E-mail Address (Internet or Uunet)

BUSINESS REPLY MAIL

FIRST CLASS MAIL   PERMIT NO. 80   SEBASTOPOL, CA

Postage will be paid by addressee

O'Reilly & Associates, Inc.

103 A Morris Street
Sebastopol CA 95472-9902

NO POSTAGE
NECESSARY IF
MAILED IN THE
UNITED STATES

BUSINESS REPLY MAIL

FIRST CLASS MAIL   PERMIT NO. 80   SEBASTOPOL, CA

Postage will be paid by addressee

O'Reilly & Associates, Inc.

103 A Morris Street
Sebastopol CA 95472-9902